The National Poetry Series established the Robert Fagles Translation Prize in 2007. This award is given annually to a translator who has shown exceptional skill in the translation of contemporary international poetry into English.

The Robert Fagles Translation Prize

2008
Lawrence Venuti, *Edward Hopper*
a translation of Catalan poet Ernest Farrés

2007
Marilyn Hacker, *King of a Hundred Horsemen*
a translation of French poet Marie Étienne

The National Poetry Series was established in 1978 to ensure the publication of poetry books annually through participating publishers. Publication is funded by the Lannan Foundation; Stephen Graham; Joyce & Seward Johnson Foundation; Glenn and Renee Schaeffer, Juliet Lea Hillman Simonds Foundation; Tiny Tiger Foundation; and Charles B. Wright III.

Edward Hopper

Other Books by Ernest Farrés

POETRY

Clavar-ne una al mall i l'altra a l'enclusa (1996)
Mosquits (1998)
Edward Hopper (2006)

EDITOR

21 poetes del XXI (2001)

Other Books by Lawrence Venuti

CRITICISM

The Translator's Invisibility: A History of Translation (2nd ed., 2008)
The Scandals of Translation: Towards an Ethics of Difference (1998)

EDITOR

Rethinking Translation: Discourse, Subjectivity, Ideology (1992)
Translation and Minority (1998)
The Translation Studies Reader (2nd ed., 2004)

TRANSLATOR

Barbara Alberti. *Delirium: A Novel.* (1980)
Aldo Rossi. *A Scientific Autobiography.* (1981)
Restless Nights: Selected Stories of Dino Buzzati. (1983)
Francesco Alberoni. *Falling in Love.* (1983)
The Siren: A Selection from Dino Buzzati. (1984)
I.U. Tarchetti. *Fantastic Tales.* (1992)
I.U. Tarchetti. *Passion: A Novel.* (1994)
Milo De Angelis. *Finite Intuition: Selected Poetry and Prose.* (1995)
J. Rodolfo Wilcock. *The Temple of Iconoclasts.* (2000)
Antonia Pozzi. *Breath: Poems and Letters.* (2002)
Italy: A Traveler's Literary Companion. (2003)
Melissa P. *100 Strokes of the Brush before Bed.* (2004)
Massimo Carlotto. *The Goodbye Kiss.* (2006)
Massimo Carlotto. *Death's Dark Abyss.* (2006)

Ernest Farrés

Edward Hopper

POEMS

□ □ □

Translated from the Catalan by Lawrence Venuti

Graywolf Press

Publication of this volume is made possible in part by a grant provided by the Minnesota State Arts Board, through an appropriation by the Minnesota State Legislature; a grant from the Wells Fargo Foundation Minnesota; and a grant from the National Endowment for the Arts, which believes that a great nation deserves great art. Significant support has also been provided by the Bush Foundation; Target; the McKnight Foundation; and other generous contributions from foundations, corporations, and individuals. To these organizations and individuals we offer our heartfelt thanks.

The Catalan texts are reproduced from Ernest Farrés's book *Edward Hopper: Cinquanta poemes sobre la seva obra pictòrica* (*Fifty poems on his pictorial work*; Barcelona: Viena, 2006). The poem that stands as the epilogue, "Sedentarisme" ("Sedentariness"), was written especially for the Princeton anthology *The Museum as Muse* (2008).

Published by Graywolf Press
250 Third Avenue North, Suite 600
Minneapolis, Minnesota 55401
All rights reserved.

www.graywolfpress.org

Published in the United States of America

ISBN 978-1-55597-544-9

2 4 6 8 9 5 3 1
First Graywolf Printing, 2009

Library of Congress Control Number: 2009926856

Cover design: Kyle G. Hunter

Cover art: Edward Hopper, 1882–1967. (*Self Portrait*), 1925–1930. Oil on canvas, 25¼ x 20⅝ in. (64.14 x 52.39 cm). Whitney Museum of American Art, New York; Josephine N. Hopper Bequest 70.1165. © Heirs of Josephine N. Hopper, licensed by the Whitney Museum of American Art. Photography by Geoffrey Clements.

Contents

Preface

The second Robert Fagles Translation Prize is awarded, after a consideration of numerous worthy submissions, and with special acknowledgment of three distinguished contestants, Elena Rivera, Fady Joudah, and Idra Novey, to Lawrence Venuti's translation of the contemporary Catalan poet Ernest Farrés's *Edward Hopper*. This work, a sequence of fifty poems, each based on a painting by the American realist artist, is not arranged chronologically according to the dates when the paintings were completed; instead the poems sketch a narrative which follows a poetic subject in transit from small-town origins to big-city life, from the search for a job to a career in art, from bachelorhood to love and companionship, from youth to age. The story belongs to Hopper, as Mr. Venuti observes, yet also to Farrés: "as the sequence unfolds, the reader discovers that the poems are also intended to be representative of social situations and historical moments, and the genre is not simply narrative, but a curious mixture of lyric and epic, complete with an invocation of the muses."

The poems do not merely rehearse the facts of the painter's life or his cantankerous opinions. The ventriloquism slips, as Mr. Venuti says, and the interrogative force of the writing constantly reminds us of the strange amalgamation of the Catalan poet and the American icon into a single being. One example must suffice, from "House by the Railroad, 1925":

> I recognize myself holding vigil
> inside a huge Victorian house,
> vacant, foreboding, phantasmagorical,
> without going crazy for what I can't possess
> yet cut off from the world, supreme example
> of original innocence.

Candor primigeni: that last phrase returns me to another happy circumstance of the choice of Mr. Venuti's splendid work besides its resourceful eloquence, its persistent vitality; in 1978 Robert Fagles published *I, Vincent*, a series of "poems from the pictures of Van Gogh," remarking that "I wanted to see if separate poems might tell a story, even a biography in small. And I wanted to try a kind of translation I hadn't done before, not from a foreign language but a group of paintings . . ." It seems such a natural way to honor not only the winner but the namesake of this prize to award the second Robert Fagles prize to Lawrence Venuti's extraordinary translation of Ernest Farrés's *Edward Hopper*, a magical if unconscious sequel to Bob Fagles's creative dream.

Richard Howard

Introduction

A contemporary Spanish poet writes a book of poems based on the paintings of a celebrated American artist, perhaps the most famous in the twentieth century. The painter's work was admitted to the artistic canon during his lifetime, and as the United States achieved international ascendancy after the Second World War, his influence stretched far and wide, evident in a broad spectrum of cultural forms and practices. The poet is bilingual, and he chose to write not in Castilian, as we might too readily expect of a Spanish citizen, but in Catalan, his mother tongue, a minor language brutally repressed under Francisco Franco's dictatorship and inevitably invested with chauvinism ever since.

How does the Catalan poet treat the American painter? With a deference commanded by prestige and power or an irreverence provoked by marginality and exclusion? How is the poet's treatment complicated by his decision to stage it as ekphrasis, the verbal representation of visual art? What unique problems are posed by translating ekphrastic poetry, where the focus of the translator's attention is not so much doubled as quadrupled, trained not only on the foreign text, but on the art work, not only on the linguistic patterns and literary traditions of the receiving culture, but on the critical reception and popular image of the artist? Perhaps most importantly, what intentions might guide a translation of Catalan poetry into English, the globally hegemonic language?

These questions ran through my mind when, in Barcelona during the spring of 2006, I happened upon Ernest Farrés's collection of poems, *Edward Hopper*. The book had won the Englantina d'Or of the Jocs Florals, a distinguished Catalan poetry prize that dates back to at least the nineteenth century, and a trickle of notices appeared in the press. I had never heard of Farrés, although he had published two previous books of poems and has long worked as a cultural editor for the Spanish-language newspaper *La Vanguardia*. Nonetheless, the international impact of an American cultural icon, the bold gesture of devoting an entire book to his mythic paintings, the ideologically charged decision to write in Catalan—these points were immediately intriguing. And they quickly became my obsessions, setting up the parameters within which I began to translate Farrés's poems.

□ □ □

Appallingly little foreign writing is Englished today. Of that amount even less consists of poetry. Every spring Poets House in New York City showcases most of the books published in the previous year, offering a comprehensive look at the American poetry scene. Translations make up a tiny fraction of total annual output, hovering between 6 and 8 percent. In 2006 approximately 1,600 books of poetry were published in the United States, but only about 100 of them were translations, more than half issued by small presses and therefore limited in print run and distribution, ultimately ephemeral.

The volume of poetry translation into English has not changed significantly since the Second World War. Nor has the hierarchy of languages from which most poetry is translated. French, Italian, German, Russian, and Spanish have long ranked at the top, followed by a regular smattering of ancient Greek and Latin and a varying number of other languages whose ranking has shifted with cultural and social developments—notably the annual announcement of the Nobel Prize for Literature, changing trends in literary taste and academic criticism, geopolitical tension, military conflict. (The other languages would include, in alphabetical order, Arabic, Chinese, Hebrew, Japanese, Polish, Sanskrit, and Swedish, among others.) And what about the range of poets and poems? 2006 saw new English versions of Homer, Sappho, Virgil, Wang Wei, *Beowulf*, Dante, Rumi, Hafiz, Hugo, Baudelaire, Pushkin, Akhmatova, Rilke, Lorca, Celan . . . A stupendous list, undoubtedly. Yet the roll call is so familiar that it reflects the utter homogeneity of prevalent tastes in foreign poetries among Anglophone readers, particularly in the United States.

Catalan has never been more than a blip on the flickering screen of literary translation in English. With little opportunity to learn about literary traditions in this language, an Anglophone reader cannot manage an appreciation of a contemporary Catalan poet that approximates the experience of an informed native reader. In the case of Ernest Farrés's *Edward Hopper*, we are not in a position to exclaim, with the Catalan poet and critic Alex Susanna, that the book is "certainly singular in the panorama of current Catalan poetry."

To choose to translate a Catalan poet, I realized, was effectively an act of linguistic and cultural ecology, a bid to preserve and bear witness to Catalan literature. To translate a Catalan poet into English, the most read language worldwide, carried further implications: it testified that the literature was deserving of translation, even at the risk of colluding with the vernacular nationalism that reemerged in Catalunya after the fall of Franco's regime. But the risk seemed worth taking. The appearance of a Catalan poet like Farrés might well cast a different light on the poetry published in English each year. It might introduce a sense of strangeness that would not be amiss in a translation, sending a signal that literary life is thriving elsewhere, not just in the English-speaking world.

□ □ □

Edward Hopper's paintings have frequently inspired Anglophone poets, British as well as American. The art historian Gail Levin, the leading authority on the artist, gathered a selection of such poems in her anthology *The Poetry of Solitude* (1995). Here the recurrent gambit is an evocative description of the visual image or a narrative suggested by the represented figures. On this basis some humanistic or social theme is explored—yet always with a detachment that reflects the poet's different time and place, different culture or social position. American poets in particular are intrigued by Hopper's paintings, but curiously they are inclined to be standoffish, rarely willing to inhabit his world.

Samuel Yellen's 1951 poem on Hopper's *Nighthawks* (1942), perhaps the first to take the painter's work as its object, is in many ways typical. The opening stanzas set the tone for what follows:

> The place is the corner of Empty and Bleak,
> The time is night's most desolate hour,
> The scene is Al's Coffee Cup or the Hamburger Tower,
> The persons in this drama do not speak.

> We who peer through that curve of plate glass
> Count three nighthawks seated there—patrons of life:
> The counterman will be with you in a jiff,
> The thick white mugs were never meant for demitasse.

For Yellen, "the single man" in the painting was once driven to play Russian roulette but "now lives out his x years' guarantee." The couple are seen as estranged after a torrid sexual encounter in which "they found/No local habitation and no name." The line alludes to the power assigned to the imagination in Shakespeare's comedy, *A Midsummer Night's Dream*, and it implies that the couple lack this faculty. The allusion also suggests that they do not share a habitation and a name in a most concrete sense: they are not married to each other, in contrast to the lovers at the end of the Shakespearean play. Marriage would then seem to represent the triumph of imagination. Hopper's couple, however, are losers.

Yellen's poem is a study in pathos, and he is the distanced observer who concludes on a note of self-congratulation:

> Oh, are we not lucky to be none of these!
> We can look on with complacent eye:
> Our satisfactions satisfy,
> Our pleasures, our pleasures please.

Can the mention of "complacent," the redundancies, the final stutter be read as ironic, hinting that the "we" is not so "lucky," after all, and therefore should not be so morally confident? Any such suggestion remains too faint to question the conservatism by which the characters are judged in the poem. The nighthawks' "pleasures" are obviously not considered authentic: they do not "please." Yellin's poem rests on the idealization of home and family that characterized mainstream American culture in the 1950s. Yet the attraction of Hopper's painting, then and now, must be due to its questioning of those values.

□ 〔〕 □

Ernest Farrés's *Edward Hopper* uniquely avoids any detachment, not only from Hopper's art and the world depicted therein, but also from his life. The poet treats the painter as his alter ego, and the poems become the site of a ventriloquist act. In the programmatic poem that opens the book, based on Hopper's *Self Portrait* (1925–1930), Farrés lays out his avowedly Borgesian premises: the painting is "a mirror," he argues, since Hopper and he "form one single person."

The project does in fact contain a biographical dimension. Although each poem takes its title from one of Hopper's paintings, Farrés does not arrange the poems chronologically according to the date when each painting was completed, as if mimicking a museum retrospective. The order is rather thematic, constructing a narrative that is discontinuous, to be sure, but nonetheless sequential. A poetic subject, an "I," moves from small-town origins to the big city, from a job search to a successful career, from bachelorhood to love and companionship, from youth to maturity, pausing at times to vacation in coastal areas.

The story belongs to Hopper, of course, who always insisted that he was just trying to paint himself. He was raised in Nyack and later settled in New York City, working as an illustrator until his paintings attracted collectors and critics, spending summers in Gloucester and Maine before building a home on Cape Cod. Farrés, however, does not precisely localize his poems, since he is also telling his own story. He grew up in the industrial town of Igualada and later moved to Barcelona, a city on the Mediterranean coast, to study at the university and to find work as a journalist.

Any biographical allusions must be inferred from titles and dates, themes and settings. For as the book unfolds the poems clearly aspire to be representative, transcending any individual life to comment on social situations and historical moments. The genre is not simply narrative, but a mixture of lyric and epic, complete with an invocation of the muses. Farrés uses Hopper's paintings to tell a story of modernity, focusing on the metropolis and its impact on personal relationships, on affect and desire. Not only does the poet share the painter's misgivings, but in poem after poem he presents them with compelling immediacy. Farrés's poem on *Nighthawks* is framed as a taut mini-drama, in which the reader eavesdrops on a couple confronting the sense that they are not "irreplaceable."

□ ▯ □

Ekphrastic literature can never be a perfect reproduction of the art that is its object. By reconstructing that object in the medium of writing, a literary work opens up a suggestive difference between the visual and the verbal, saying what cannot be seen, a saying that prompts a different kind of seeing. Even when motivated by admiration, even when taking the form of careful description, ekphrasis engages in an emulative rivalry that borders on critique—and sometimes plunges into it, possibly without the writer's awareness.

Farrés's poems tend not to describe. Instead they freely speculate, using Hopper's paintings as springboards for reflection and invention. In *Railroad*

Sunset, 1929 surreal colors are detached from the "polychrome sky" and deepened with literary allusion. In *Hotel Room, 1931* the sense of sight is joined by smell, the life of the solitary female figure is inserted into a planetary time scheme, and the room where she sits expands to cosmic proportions. Occasionally, Farrés tampers with the realist illusion in poetry as well as painting by insisting on the artifice of the image. After offering a verisimilar account of the landscape, *Cape Cod Sunset, 1934* names the shades of paint on the artist's palette, while *Cape Cod Evening, 1939* refers to shadows as "smudges." At times, the recurrent biographical motif can introduce a jolting detail. Lizards inhabit Catalunya, not Cape Cod; olive groves are found in Spain, not New York or New England.

By the same token, Farrés's poems do not merely rehearse the facts of the painter's life or his cantankerous opinions. Hopper's politics, for instance, were extremely conservative. Not only did he oppose Franklin Delano Roosevelt's presidency, but he was critical of the Depression-era Federal Art Project, which employed his teachers and associates, realist painters such as John Sloan and Raphael Soyer. Always the romantic individualist, Hopper felt that government funding compromised the artist's independence and led to second-rate work. Farrés, like Hopper, criticizes modern cultural and social developments. But the painter would not have resorted to the marxist-oriented sociological analysis that recurs in poems like *The City, 1927* and *New York Office, 1962*. At these points, the ventriloquism slips, and the poetic voice reflects a contemporary European sensibility.

Farrés glances at these discrepancies in his poem on the *Self Portrait*. "If Goethe was reincarnated in Kafka," he imagines, "Hopper in a transmigration most apt/pulled it off in me." An ekphrastic work always transforms the visual image it represents by inscribing a distinctively literary interpretation. Yet Farrés's analogy suggests an interpretation that, far from being noncommittal or innocent, is potentially interrogative. If Goethe, at once classical and romantic, metamorphosed into the absurdist Kafka, we might expect Farrés to give an ironic twist to Hopper's uncanny realism. In the case of the most voyeuristic paintings, such as *Compartment C, Car 293* (1938) and *Night Windows* (1928), Farrés need only situate them in a narrative to expose the hidden conditions of the image, the male gaze turning the female figures into objects of desire.

□ ▯ □

Farrés's use of Catalan poses special challenges to the translator. His poems combine the current standard dialect of the language with colloquialisms and slang, poetical archaisms, academic and technical jargons, foreign loan words. He frequently includes the idiomatic expressions in which Catalan is abundant, as well as clichés from elite and popular culture. In my translations I have sought to match this heterogeneity, both at the precise points where Farrés's poems cultivate it and, whenever I could not, at other points where his Catalan is in the standard dialect.

Yet the English of my translations goes much further. Taking my cue from the biographical dimension of Farrés's project, I develop an American vernacular that samples the speech and writing of Hopper and his wife, the painter Josephine Nivison Hopper. Although famously laconic, averse to speaking in public, likely to find writing sheer drudgery, Hopper spoke and wrote a particularly rich form of American English. He routinely mixed registers and styles, formal and colloquial, poetical and slangy, evoking a wide variety of cultural discourses. His language can sometimes be linked to certain periods in the twentieth century, even specific decades, establishing a veritable chronology of American culture. I scoured whatever documents survived Hopper and Nivison and assembled a lexicon of representative words and phrases, which I used in the translations where I could create a semantic correspondence with the Catalan texts.

My work is translation, not adaptation, even if in some instances it edges towards what poets today might call a "version." Nor, I would argue, does the American English result in a questionable domestication. On the contrary, my decision to weave Hopper's own language into the translations invites the reader to foreground what is different in Farrés's treatment of the paintings, in his very themes, extending the interrogative force of the writing. The translations aim to defamiliarize the Americanness of the language as well as the work of a canonical painter. In the process, however, questions may also be raised about the Catalan poet's peculiar relationship to American culture, admiringly dependent yet critically autonomous.

□ ▯ □

Perhaps the most difficult problem confronting the translator is how to compensate for the violence of translating: the sheer loss of the multiple contexts in which the foreign work originated and which always inform the foreign reader's experience of it. These contexts are print and electronic, linguistic and literary, cultural and social. They range from the connotations of specific words to literary traditions and contemporary trends to the copy that appears on the book cover to the reviews and blogs that greet the book upon publication—all in the foreign language and culture. Because translating displaces these contexts, the notion that it can enable an equivalent effect is a hoax. A reader of a translation can never appreciate it with quite the same breadth and depth of reference that figure in the foreign reader's appreciation of the foreign work.

Nevertheless, the vacuum is automatically filled with previous cultural experiences, which create a set of comparable but markedly different contexts in the receiving situation. The translator must be prepared for this crucial difference, for the drift to what is more familiar to the reader, for the relentlessly ethnocentric movement that lies at the heart of translating. In the case of cultures that translate relatively little, like the United States, and of literatures that have been relatively neglected, like Catalan, the problem is exacerbated to an impossible degree. Still, it can be anticipated and addressed in the translating, I believe, if not resolved to the satisfaction of every potential readership.

Take the very sound of the foreign language, its prosody, always stripped away in the move to the translating language. With poetry, this loss matters a great deal because rhythms are meaningful, poetic meters bear the weight of literary tradition, and readers develop an auditory imagination on the basis of previous listening exeriences. In Catalan, two meters have accrued the greatest literary value: the decasyllabic and the alexandrine. Farrés is mindful of this historical fact while avoiding rhyme for a prosaic tone that better fits his exploration of modern society. He divides his book into roughly two metrical halves that underwrite the biographical narrative, moving from mixed, syncopated rhythms suggestive of youthful vitality to more consistent, traditional meters that signal a sedate maturity.

Because English literary traditions are dominated by iambic pentameter, comparable results can be achieved only by experimenting with various forms of blank verse, Shakespearean, Miltonic, Wordsworthian. This I have attempted, although not without varying the number of stresses in the line. Whereas Farrés's lines are always metrical, even when an individual poem uses different meters, I have at places resorted to free verse, attending to the resonance of line breaks, their ability to parse syntax and to annotate meaning. As my heterogeneous, Hopper-inflected English jostles against the traditional meters and the conversational rhythms, the effects run the gamut from prose-like fluency to quiet lyricism, from magniloquence to amusing parody, at times matching the Catalan texts, at others unavoidably diverging from them.

In the transition to English, Farrés's *Edward Hopper* comes to be positioned in another set of contexts—linguistic and literary, art historical and biographical—to replace the Catalan ones that are irreparably lost for Anglophone readers. You are likely to bring to my translation not only a wealth of previous encounters with English-language poetries, but a familiarity with Hopper's paintings and perhaps some acquaintance with the poems that have been written in response to them. In an effort to support and enrich this sort of reading, I have created a section of endnotes that incorporate information about the lives of the painter and the poet as well as about their work. Against this backdrop, Farrés's book of poems proves to be remarkable in its ambitiousness, its wit, and its probing interpretations of the visual images.

Lawrence Venuti

Edward Hopper

Self Portrait, 1925–1930

On escric tot aquest assortiment de versos
    hi ha de fet l'Edward Hopper que els engendra
    i que, bo i transcendint l'espai-temps, ve a donar-me
    les consignes.
             El seu autoretrat
és, com li agradaria al fantasista Borges,
    un mirall que reprodueix no tant
    el rostre del pintor com el reflex estàtic
    de la meva imatge. Podem ben creure-ho:
Hopper i jo formem una sola persona.

    El seu posat tranquil i seriós,
    les corbes de la cara o els tips d'embadalir-se
    que s'han fet els seus ulls sense cap dubte
m'incumbeixen. Si Goethe es reencarnà en Kafka,
    Hopper en una transmigració
    plena d'encert ho féu en mi i així, prenent
    el cos d'un poeta, aconseguirà
que el seu llegat artístic es prolongui en el temps
    (al final només resta la paraula,
    la poesia).
             L'home del quadre ja no és
    aquell pintor prim com un tel de ceba
que va venir de jove a Europa a trencar el glaç,
    sinó el pintor casat, de vida estable,
    que mostrarà el seu món personal reflectint
    profusament ciutats, paisatges, dones.
("No faig," va dir, "sinó pintar-me a mi mateix.")
    Erra qui veu representacions
    d'Amèrica del Nord on de debò bateguen
    els tràfecs de la solitud humana,
on intuïm les pors, obsessions, neguits,
    dilemes o estats d'ànim de l'artista
    i hi apareix la Jo, l'omnipresent esposa.
    Com la pintura emmarcada, també
les abundants finestres i portes són miralls.

Self Portrait, 1925–1930

On the spot where I write all this hodgepodge of verses
    stands Edward Hopper, in fact, who engenders them
    and who, neatly transcending space-time, sends me
    the signals.
                His self-portrait creates,
as would bring delight to Borges the fantasist,
    a mirror that reproduces not so much
    the painter's face as the static reflection
    of my image. Make no bones about it:
Hopper and I form one single person.

    His pose, relaxed and sober,
    the curves of the face, the surfeit of enchantment
    that shaped his eyes without a doubt
show my concerns. If Goethe was reincarnated in Kafka,
    Hopper in a transmigration most apt
    pulled it off in me and thus, assuming
    a poet's body, he will succeed
in extending his artistic legacy in time
    (in the end, only the word remains,
    poetry).
                The man in the picture no longer is
    that painter thin as a sliver of onion
who came to Europe young to break the ice,
    but the married painter, his life settled,
    who will exhibit his personal world profusely
    reflecting cities, landscapes, women.
("I'm just trying to paint myself," he said.)
    You're off the track to see representations
    of North America where what really stirs
    is the agitation of human solitude,
where we intuit the fears, obsessions, anxieties,
    dilemmas or states of mind of the artist
    and Jo appears, the omnipresent wife.
    Like the framed painting, the scads
of windows and doors are mirrors too.

"No faig sinó pintar-me a mi mateix."
No expressen els poetes el seu pensament propi?
Condemnat tot a ser una sola cosa,
en un ésser vivent vam fondre'ns ell i jo:
els seus neguits o estats d'ànim són meus
i a la vegada els meus són de tots a la llum
d'una mateixa lluna arreu del món.

"I'm just trying to paint myself."
Don't poets express their own thoughts?
With all and sundry condemned to be a single thing,
he and I were fused in a living creature:
     his anxieties and states of mind are mine
     and mine, in the same breath, belong to everybody
     in the light of the same moon all over the world.

Stairway, 1949

Quin coi d'escriptor seré si toco el dos
i, després d'haver tastat el bo i dolent,
no em veig amb cor de donar-ne testimoni?
Pel que pugui ser, no aneu amb mitges tintes
i inspireu-me, filles de Zeus i Mnemòsine,
una poesia que no concedeixi
el benefici del dubte, que reculli
pensaments profunds i que faci que el món
aquest, tan inescrutable, sembli clar.
Que, com una clau al pany, obri les portes
a l'aire vivificant i al safareig.
Que, com una ona expansiva, es dissemini
fins als escorrancs dels turons.
                              Megalòmanes
muses gregues, aclariu-me què cal fer
per fixar amb paraules incontrovertibles
el sistema de bellesa dels paisatges
i dels dies amb les albes i foscants
i de les nits amb les llunes i penombres
i així mateix l'espectacle de la gent
i el desmanec de les àrees urbanes
i l'encís de les societats modernes.

En lloc de mirar la televisió
o d'estar-vos amb les mans a les butxaques,
no em deixeu tirat i encomaneu-me el nervi
per copsar les meravelles de la vida.
Ara baixaré les escales que donen
a l'exterior i no penso defraudar.

Stairway, 1949

What a crappy poet I'd be if I scrammed
and after sampling the really nasty bits
didn't feel up to making my deposition.
Because this could happen, don't go halfway,
daughters of Zeus and Mnemosyne, inspire
in me a poetry that doesn't concede
the benefit of the doubt, that scrapes together
profound thoughts and enables this our world,
so inscrutable, to seem transparent.
That like a key in a lock can open doors
to a quickening wind as well as the laundry room.
That like an expansive wave extends its reach
o'er hill and dale.
                    Megalomaniac
Greek muses, clarify what must be done
so as to fix in incontrovertible words
the aesthetic principle of landscapes
and days with dawns and dusks
and nights with moons and penumbras
and, even so, the spectacle of the populace
and urban areas in disarray
and the sorcery of modern societies.

Instead of watching television
or standing around with your hands in your pockets,
don't abandon my plan and give me the nerve
to grasp the wonders of life.
Now I'll descend the stairs that lead outside
and not worry about letting anybody down.

Small Town Station, 1918–1920

Jo i somnis on germinen
futurs amb fites-per-les-quals-lluitar.
No sense esforç, altra vegada jo
i tempteigs indubtables
d'iniciar una història.
Raspallets de les dents
i pastes dentifrícies
per refrescar l'alè.
Dreceres per fer cap
a les estacions i banys de llum. Blavors
de corniols i blavors de xicrandes.
Llistons més baixos i llistons més alts.
Vents que expandeixen els estratocúmuls
i vents que els escombren pengim-penjam.
Gats escàpols i carrerons mig morts
als nuclis de població petits.
Morositats i tantsemenfotismes.
Mmm . . . que estrany que és anar-se'n (i que estrany que és no fer-ho).
Enrenous-enrenous i silencis-silencis.
Moviments de canell i repataneries.
Tres quarts menys cinc, tres quarts en punt, tres quarts i cinc.
Maletes a l'andana i burilles per terra.
Valors morals i càmeres de seguretat. Tot
un revoltim de rostres acaliuats i béns
de consum que no haurien d'anomenar-se així.
I, algun dia, tu i jo.

Small Town Station, 1918–1920

Me and dreams where futures bud
with milestones-to-grind-for.
Not without strain, me again
and the irrefutable trial and error
of getting a life.
Toothbrushes
and toothpaste
to freshen up the breath.
Shortcuts that head straight
to stations and pools of light. The blue
of columbine and the blue of jacaranda.
One bar is set lower, another higher.
Winds that swell the stratocumulus
and winds that sweep them away clumsy-like.
Stray cats and dead alleys
in the tiny center of town.
Sluggishness and couldn'tgiveadamnism.
Hmmm . . . how strange to leave (and not to leave).
Hustle-bustle and hush-hush.
Wrist movements and digging in the heels.
Twenty to, a quarter, ten.
Luggage on the platform and cigarette butts on the ground.
Moral values and security cameras. A whole
jumble of incandescent faces and consumer
goods (which I shouldn't like to be called that).
And, some day, you and me.

Railroad Train, 1908

Tan aviat com el vagó de cua
es perd de vista, ja
s'han oblidat de tu.
És com caure del candeler o com treure'ls
un pes de sobre. Així
ells, que no toquen quarts
ni hores ni faran res
a la vida, se'n renten
les mans. Entesos. Però els trens que agafes
són decidits, climatitzats, carnívors,
de bona soca. Emblanquidores boires
pugnen sense èxit per intimidar-los.
Inspiren, expiren, s'irisen, bullen.
Necessiten un fotimer d'espai
per levitar apressadament amb rumb
a la possibilitat-d'altres-mons
o un ordre-extraordinari-de-coses.
Mostren, les seves finestretes, valls
i collades.
        És típic marxar en dies de cel
plomís, com si es formessin els núvols pel contacte
amb la suor i l'alè calents.
              Hores més tard
t'embolcallaran ombres i llums noves, ventades
i colors canviants, insòlites bullícies.

Railroad Train, 1908

No sooner is the caboose
out of sight than they've
already forgotten you.
It's like losing clout or taking
a load off their minds. That's just
how they, who are out
to lunch or do nothing
with their lives, wash their hands
of you. Got it? Yet the trains you catch
are determined, air-conditioned, carnivorous,
in fine fettle. Thickening fogs
rise yet fail to intimidate them.
They breathe in, breathe out, iridesce, seethe.
They need a ton of room
to levitate in a hurry, heading
for the possibility of other worlds
or an extraordinary order of things.
Their windows give evidence of valleys,
depressions.
         Leaving on days beneath a leaden sky
is true to type, as if clouds were formed through contact
with sweat and hot breath.
            Hours later
you'll be swaddled in strange lights and shadows,
gusts and twittering colors, unaccustomed racket.

House by the Railroad, 1925

Fantasiejo que la sort se'm posa
a l'abast. Ara bé: hi ha sorts diverses. Hi ha,
posem per cas, aquelles que apareixen ad hoc
i aquelles que es despleguen
a recules. Hi ha dèficits de sort i superàvits
de sort. D'igual manera, tenim la bona-sort,
la sort-del-dia-a-dia, la sort-sense-memòria
i la mala-sort, dita també malastrugança.
Hi ha sorts que són un peix que es porta l'oli i sorts
que són àspids, escórpores, porcs senglars i estornells.
Tinc una visió de vies mig cobertes
d'herba i rovell llançant-se,
com un traç tosc o un tall
amb irisacions que agafen per sorpresa,
contra un demà sense taló d'Aquil·les.
I m'imagino qui-sap-les planures
i serres lliures de la mà de l'home
i encara no impermeabilitzades
a la mercè del cerç, l'aiguat o la calor.
Però les fantasies no s'aturen aquí.
Com l'esqueix d'un record de la vida passada,
una altra fantasia que em sotraga la ment
és aquella en què em reconec en vetlla
dins una gran casa victoriana,
buida, feréstega, fantasmagòrica,
sense delir-me pel que no tindré
però desvinculat del món, suprem exemple
del candor primigeni.

House by the Railroad, 1925

I fantasize that luck is placed
within my reach. Of course, there's different kinds.
Take the kind that turns up ad hoc, for instance,
and the kind that unfolds
backwards. There are deficits and surpluses
of luck. By the same token, we have good luck,
everyday luck, luck-you-don't-remember,
and bad luck, a.k.a. misfortune.
Luck that puts us on easy street and luck
that's an asp, a scorpion fish, a wild boar, a starling.
I have a vision of train tracks half covered
with grass and rust, hurling themselves—
like a jagged line or a blade
with an iridescence that catches you by surprise—
against a tomorrow without an Achilles heel.
And I imagine who-knows-what plains
and mountains untouched by human hand
and still not weatherproofed
at the mercy of nor'easters, downpours, and heat.
But the fantasies don't stop here.
Like the rip in a memory of a past life,
another jolts my mind:
I recognize myself holding vigil
inside a huge Victorian house,
vacant, foreboding, phantasmagorical,
without going crazy for what I can't possess
yet cut off from the world, supreme example
of original innocence.

Railroad Sunset, 1929

Mentre declina el dia,
esmerlits núvols dissipant-se pengen
del cel policromat pel cantó de ponent.

El tros cobert de blau és d'un blau com Ulisses,
com l'atmosfera, com uns ulls turquesa
que s'alcen com el sol o com l'aigua que surt
de mare. Pel que concerneix el groc,
aquest té l'aura de les "grans conquestes."
És grogor de tremuja
de sembradora, de camp de rostoll
o de lluna rajant com mel de romaní.
A sota, la tonalitat vermella
podria evocar cirerers en flor,
maneres-porprades-de-ser-feliços
o peixos a l'aljub.

Es desfà el muntanyam
de l'horitzó en replecs
verdosos com la fullaraca o l'herba
del jardí i, a tocar,
es retallen les vies
fosforescents del tren
sobre un fons que, enfosquit
per la posta, és tan negre
com un mal averany
o com el grall d'un corb.

Railroad Sunset, 1929

As the day draws to a close,
gaunt, fading clouds hang
in the western corner of the polychrome sky.

The patch covered with blue is a blue like Ulysses,
like the atmosphere, like turquoise eyes
that rise like the sun or like water brimming
over. Respecting the yellow,
it is suffused with the aura of great conquests.
It is the yellowness of a grain
hopper, a stubble field
or a moon flowing like rosemary honey.
Below, the shade of red
could evoke cherry trees in flower,
purple-ways-of-being-happy
or fish in a tank.

The mountain ridge dissolves
on the horizon in greenish
folds like fallen leaves or grass
in a garden and hard by
the phosphorescent train
tracks are limned
on a ground that, darkened
by sundown, is as black
as an ill omen
or the deep croak of a raven.

Compartment C, Car 293, 1938

Rostre sever, cabells
més o menys rossos, ulls
amb una espurna d'introversió,
cutis al pic de la vida, posat
de ves-guipant-me-fins-que-t'avorreixis,
vestit negre que li estrenyia els pits
i un joc de cames llargues i en plenes facultats,
era, i fa de bon dir, una dona atractiva
i, en el sentit modern del mot, "independent."

Aquelles hores mortes del tren eren propícies
per llançar-li mirades furtives a la dona
que seia a l'altra banda del passadís. Llegia,
la pobra, amb tanta concentració
que a l'horabaixa li passà per alt
que els últims raigs del sol s'adherien encesos
per l'oest a la volta sense límits del cel.

Compartment C, Car 293, 1938

Face stern, hair
more or less blonde, eyes
with an inward-looking glint,
skin in the pink, wearing
a stare-till-you're-bored attitude
in a black dress that hugged her breasts
and a pair of long legs, in good working order,
she looked real swell, sure enough,
and "independent," as the saying goes.

The down time on the train was just
the ticket for stealing looks at her
as she sat across the aisle, reading—
poor kid—with such concentration
that at dusk she completely missed
the sun's last rays burning in the west,
stuck to the limitless vault of the sky.

Approaching a City, 1946

Veig terres rònegues i alguns pinars
que m'acompanyen llargament (amb signes
de presència humana
propera) a la meitat
d'un temps anticiclònic.

Creix a mesura que avancem el nombre
d'edificis industrials que s'alcen
com moles de desmoralitzadora
i encomanadissa lletjor i, al lluny,
hi ha la ciutat superpoblada, amb ínfules
de bastidor d'un espectacle empíric,
desproveïda de sentit comú,
calidoscòpica.
              Veig regadius,
panells publicitaris
i ponts que salven recs
i carreteres entortolligant-se.

Veig els murs de contenció guixats
amb esprais de colors que separen les vies
de l'imbricat continuum de carrers, magatzems
i cases puntejades d'esquifides finestres.

Com si es tractés d'un tràveling, la càmera s'acosta
a la boca del túnel i, en el moment d'entrar-hi
i veure el món present desnaturalitzat
i de sobte confós amb la foscor novella,
em sento com qui es fica on no el demanen, deixo
emportar-me pels nervis i penso si faig bé.

Approaching a City, 1946

I see scrub lands and some pine groves
that escort me for a long stretch (with signs
of human presence
nearby) in the midst
of anticyclonic weather.

It increases at the rate we advance
the number of industrial buildings that rise
like huge masses of demoralizing
and contagious ugliness, and in the distance
looms the overpopulated city, with infulae
of framework for an empiricist spectacle,
bereft of common sense,
kaleidoscopic.
                        I see irrigated lands,
billboards and bridges
spanning ditches
and twisting highways.

I see retaining walls with spray-painted
scrawls dividing routes
in the overlapping continuum of streets, warehouses
and homes dotted with narrow windows.

As if rigged for a tracking shot, the camera approaches
the mouth of the tunnel and just at the moment of entry,
seeing the present denatured world
and suddenly overwhelmed by unfamiliar darkness,
I feel like someone sticking his nose where it don't belong.
I let myself get carried away with jitters and think
that's all right.

The City, 1927

Amb pagesia pobra
i lumpenproletariat i classes
treballadores que penosament
van prosperar fins a sortir del pou
es construeixen les nostres històries
familiars, històries que són el viu reflex
del nostre temps. Sorgits del "vulgus," formem part
de les capes mitjanes, siguin mitjanes-baixes
o més acomodades, del món d'avui. Nou-rics,
individualistes i desmemoriats,
queda palès que estem en disposició
d'aconseguir més èxits materials i viure
la vida a fons. Em sento cridat a ser un d'aquests,
a treballar a preu fet i a pensar-me-les totes.
Arribo a la ciutat per raons de treball.
No puc dissimular el meu entusiasme.

He viscut molta vida (sense amb prou feines viure-la)
i en viuré molta més (perquè la vida és llarga).
Les nostres vides prenen un ritme trepidant.
Les restes dels naufragis no compten en una època
de falses referències i canvis successius.
Les oportunitats s'aprofiten o passen
de llarg. Quan menys s'espera, deixem de ser el que fórem
i oblidem el que havíem après.
                              Fet i pastat
com tothom, discretíssim, un-de-tants, no aparento
sorpresa ni accelero la respiració.

Al cor, al moll de l'os, al mig d'una espiral
de subjectes el·líptics, escenes coloristes
i probabilitats estadísticament
demostrables de "caure abans d'alçar-me," em mostro
segur de mi mateix, em fico la camisa
per dins dels pantalons i m'implico de ple.

The City, 1927

With dirt-poor peasantry,
lumpenproletariat, and working
stiffs who arduously
prospered till they got out of the hole
our family histories are constructed,
histories that are "the living reflection
of our times." Sprung from the vulgus, we form
the middle strata today, petty bourgeois
or better off. Nouveaux riches, individualists,
the amnesic, we're better positioned
to make a killing, clearly, and live
life to the hilt. I feel called to take my place,
to work for a wage and pursue every angle.
I arrive in the city to hunt for a job.
I can't disguise how het-up I am.

I've lived a lot (just scratching the surface)
and I'll live much more (for ever and a day).
Our lives assume a frenetic pace.
The scraps from the shipwrecks don't count
in an era of false reports and serial change.
Opportunities are exploited or slip away.
When less is expected, we stop being what we were
and afterwards forget what we had.
                                        The spitting image
of everyman, discreet, a-face-in-the-crowd, I show
no surprise and don't breathe any faster.

Deep down, in the very marrow, amidst a whorl
of elliptical subjects, colorful scenes
and statistically demonstrable
probabilities of sinking-before-rising, I appear
sure of myself. I tuck my shirt
inside my pants, and I'm directly implicated.

Mira que n'és, de gran, la ciutat d'esperit
eclèctic, el transsumpte del vell Cafarnaüm,
el can penja-i-despenja on la llei de l'oferta
i la demanda es troba en el seu element.
Tendes de comestibles, fàbriques en desús,
places en obres i carrers coberts
amb un vel de monòxid de carboni, la mística
del gregarisme i de les hores punta,
el sol que reverbera en finestres d'immobles
de finals del XIX que surten a subhasta,
altes arquitectures futuristes i blocs
de pisos sense personalitat,
oliveres de rabassudes soques
que fructifiquen a les acaballes
de la tardor, diversitat de pins
(blancs i negres i pinyoners) frisosos
per tocar el cel, alzines
de capçades espesses,
plàtans ornamentals
que em faran sentir còmode,
gairebé com a casa.

See how grand the city is with its spirit
eclectic, the copy of old Capharnum,
the bazaar where the law of supply
and demand is found in its element.
Grocery stores, abandoned factories,
construction sites, streets covered
by a shroud of carbon monoxide,
the mysticism of sociability and rush hours,
the sun shimmering on windows
of fin-de-siècle estates up for auction,
towering futuristic architecture
and characterless apartment blocks,
olive groves cleared of stumps
yielding a crop in the last days
of fall, an assortment of pines
(white and dark and nut-bearing)
anxious to touch the sky,
oaks with dense branches,
ornamental plane trees
that make me feel comfortable,
almost as if I were home.

Shakespeare at Dusk, 1935

Aquell matí, en despertar-se d'un somni
enrevessat, es va trobar al seu llit
convertit en un monstruós insecte,
però es llevà corrents
i se n'anà a la feina.
Tants fatics, tanta lluita,
tantes penes, tants maldecaps, tants tràngols,
tants cavalls de batalla, tantes privacions,
tantes desavinences i tantes males cares
deriven de "complir les obligacions
laborals" refregant-se, com un cabdell baldat
i a tota màquina, per terra. Gotes
de suor li rajaren de les bellugadisses
potetes i de la còrpora negra,
va entrar en un estat permanent d'estrès,
s'esmalucà i no podia valer-se.
Si un trastorn maníaco-depressiu
comporta una rotació d'eufòries
i llanguiments, la incorporació
mental i física al món del treball
dividí en ombres i llums el seu ésser,
deixant-li un interstici entre ambdues meitats
on un resquitx de seny hi tenia cabuda.

Així, doncs, aquell vespre, en plegar de la feina,
el titil·lant attrezzo de l'urbs el forçaria
a aclarir-se la vista i a reptar pam a pam
pel paviment, de camí cap a casa.
Com un actor que acaba creient-se el seu paper,
com un convers a la religió
"dels que manen," es va trobar en un parc
convertit en camaleó ullerós,
malhumorat i embegut d'endorfines.
A l'entorn, ginkgos, parterres i estàtues

Shakespeare at Dusk, 1935

That morning, on waking from a troubled
dream, he found himself in bed
transformed into a monstrous insect,
but he rose in a hurry
and went to the office.
So much effort, struggle,
suffering, worry, distress,
obsession, privation,
friction and sourness
derive from "fulfilling work
obligations," manically dragging
oneself through the mud
like a frazzled ball of yarn. Drops
of sweat flowed from his fidgety
little legs and black body. He
entered a permanent state of stress,
dislocated a hip and couldn't manage.
If a manic-depressive disorder
involves a rotation of euphorias
and lethargies, his mental and physical
embodiment in the world of work
split his being into lights and shadows,
leaving a crack between two halves
where a modicum of sense was wedged.

And so, when he knocked off that evening,
the glittering mise-en-scène of the city forced him
to brighten his outlook and crawl along
the pavement inch by inch the whole way home.
Like an actor who winds up believing his role,
like a convert to the religion
of those in charge, he found himself in a park
transformed into a chameleon with ringed eyes,
peevish and saturated with endorphins.
All around, ginkgos, flower beds and statues

profanes feien com aquell qui res
a la claror de l'ocàs i els anuncis
lluminosos. Per un instant l'udol
d'una sirena interrompé el silenci
i s'allunyà ràpidament. Havien
de venir més dificultats, ensurts,
canvis i la comprensió final
que el camí pres no tenia dreceres.

profane were acting like nothing special
in the radiance of sunset and illuminated
signs. For a moment, the howl
of a siren broke the silence
and rapidly receded. More troubles
were sure to come, scares, changes,
and the final realization
that the road taken offers no shortcuts.

East River, c. 1920–1923

La més gran influència
    que la lectura de *Siddharta*
    exercí sobre meu
    tingué molt a veure amb els rius.
D'ençà d'aquell moment
    van adquirir un significat
    més pregon i simbòlic.
    Fa temps que jugo amb l'avantatge
de saber que vivim dins un somni i que aquest
    no acaba mai. Em refereixo a un somni urbà amb tot d'edificis,
    de carburants, de tes aromàtics de menta,
    de fàbriques tèxtils, de fàbriques on s'adoben pells i d'un riu
que reflecteix el fort del crepuscle i provoca
    un estrany efecte catàrtic i alliberador. La ciutat
    instaura lleis i els rius són els rebels que malden
    per desobeir-les (per bé que poques vegades se'n surtin).

Tot riu és una mena
    de somni encabit en el somni
    més global de la vida
    i, de pas, s'assembla a nosaltres:
descendeix de molt lluny
    a bots i empentes, es difon
    i encarna l'esperit
    d'allò-que-podria-haver-estat.

East River, c. 1920–1923

The greatest influence
      my reading of *Siddhartha*
      exercised on me
      had much to do with rivers.
Ever since that moment
      they acquired a meaning
      most profound and symbolic.
      For a while I've played with the edge
of knowing we live in a never-ending
      dream. I refer to an urban dream jam-packed
      with buildings, hydrocarbons, aromatic mint teas,
      textile factories, tanneries, and a river
that reflects the essence of dusk and provokes
      a weird effect, cathartic and liberating. The city
      institutes laws and rivers are rebels that try their damndest
      to break them (although they rarely get away with it).

Every river is a type
      of dream that lies inside
      a more global dream of life,
      and flowing it resembles us:
descending from pretty far away
      by fits and starts, it disseminates
      and embodies the spirit
      of what could have been.

Early Sunday Morning, 1930

Som al 1930 i és diumenge al matí,
d'hora. Ensonyat encara, enfilo una avinguda
i tot està inactiu i no hi ha vianants
a la vista. L'entenc, aquest apregonar-se
en tanta quietud, com una anomalia
en el campi-qui-pugui diari, si bé em plau
com plauen les rareses, les gangues, els crepuscles.

Flanquejat per inerts edificis, sumit
en el gorg del silenci i a gust amb mi mateix,
em trobo caminant tot sol com en un somni.
Tributari del lleure, ni que sigui només
durant un clar matí de diumenge, esdevinc
un nen que arrenca el pas cap a un temps molt més pròsper
(el nen que tal vegada vaig ser en un temps llunyà),
un nouvingut badoc que exulta amb el poquíssim
que ha vist com si estigués als llimbs, el personatge
central d'un vell llibrot que duria per títol
Vicissituds d'un pobre però viu roda-soques
i de com va rodar per topants pintorescos
a la bona de Déu i sense avergonyir-se'n
o un content demiürg que omple de rebombori
els cafès, barberies i botigues tancades
i de tropell de gent l'avinguda deserta
que trepitjo.
        La "fi del món" diferirà
ben poc d'un escenari tan buit.
                A Baudelaire
li vindria de nou reaparèixer aquí
i invocaria allaus humanes i el retruny
dels carrers.
        Tot això té pinta d'emboscada,
ho admeto. Per la forma que tinc de passejar,

Early Sunday Morning, 1930

Still sleepy, I slip down an avenue.
Everything is dormant without a soul
in sight. I register this immersion
in so much stillness as a freak
in the daily every-man-for-himself,
even though I'm tickled pink
like it was a rarity, a windfall, or a sunset.

Flanked by lifeless buildings, plunged
in the pool of silence, pleased with myself,
I'm walking all alone as in a dream.
Tributary to leisure, even if only
on a bright Sunday morning, I become
a child starting out at a much more propitious time
(the child I was perhaps many years ago),
a curious newcomer who revels in the least little thing
he's seen as if he didn't have a clue, the main
character of a fat old book that bears the title
The Vicissitudes of a Poor but Nimble Drifter
and How He Roamed through Picturesque Lands
By the Grace of God and Without Shame
or some happy demiurge who raises a ruckus
in closed cafès, barber's, and shops
filling the deserted avenue where I walk
with a throng of people.
                    The end of the world won't differ
much from a stage so empty.
                    Baudelaire
would be flabbergasted to come back to life here:
he'd invoke the human onrush and the thunder
of the streets.
                    The whole thing looks like an ambush,
I admit. Given the way I comport myself,

endiumenjat i apàtic, algú que m'espiés
ajupit com un enze darrere una finestra
encara em confondria amb una ànima errant,
un boc expiatori o una encarnació
del mal. Sense immutar-me, faré com qui sent ploure.

spiffed up and spunkless, anybody who spots me
crouched like some idler behind a window
might just confuse me with a wandering spirit,
a scapegoat or incarnation
of evil. Unflustered, I'll turn a deaf ear.

Manhattan Bridge Loop, 1928

Res del que succeeix succeeix perquè sí.
Hi ha una "raó" que alena en l'aire, en les llambordes,
en els balls o en les flors morades del safrà.

En aquesta vorera va vomitar-hi algú,
anit, o abans-d'ahir pel cap alt. Els carrers
són goluts i confisquen el que poden, brutícia
d'aquella-que-arrepleguen-escombrant i corrues
de formigues, pedretes i el fullam sec que agita
el vent. Així és com busco, posant-hi atenció,
les explicacions de la realitat,
el fonament darrer "del que passa," la cèl·lula
endògena o l'escorç a plena llum del dia,
talment com si ens busquéssim (amb compte) els uns als altres.

Llueix, per Sant Martí, un sol electritzant.
Una faixa de cirrus decorativa talla
el cel en dos (del cel al terra on poso els peus
tot és fet de ferides incisivo-contuses
i de nuesa). Miro també un grup d'homes grans
i els rostres de trets durs dels forasters que em guaiten
com si a la samarreta portés els gira-sols
de Van Gogh. Una línia de visió boirosa
alterna amb perspectives més clares, els coloms
amb el conglomerat urbà i el darwinisme
amb els girs personals dins un marc que molts jutgen
severament. Un rrrrrr cacofònic ressona
a les meves orelles i mai no es fa el silenci;
no pas zzzzzz, sinó el rrrrrr que mou un milió
de persones posades d'acord per fer cridòria.

Manhattan Bridge Loop, 1928

Nothing that happens happens just because.
There's a reason that breathes in the air, in cobblestones,
in dances and the purple flowers of saffron.

Someone vomited on this sidewalk during the night,
or the day before yesterday at the most. The streets
are gluttonous and confiscate what they can, dirt
from whatever is swept together and lines
of ants, pebbles and dry leaves stirred
by wind. Thus paying careful attention I search
for explanations of reality,
the foundation beneath "what comes to pass," the cell
endogenous or foreshortening in broad daylight,
precisely as if we were searching (with care) for one another.

An electrifying sun blazes, courtesy of Sant Martí.
A decorative strip of cirrus slices
the sky in two (from sky to ground, where I lay my feet,
everything is composed of cut-bruised wounds
and bareness). I also eye a bunch of old men
and the hard faces of strangers who watch me
as if I wore a T-shirt printed with sunflowers
by Van Gogh. A hazy line of sight
alternates with sharper perspectives, pigeons
with the urban conglomerate, darwinism
with personal spins inside a frame that many
judge harshly. A cacophonous rrrrrr resounds
in my ears without ever growing silent;
not zzzzzz, but the rrrrrr that moves a million
people who've reached an agreement to raise hell.

The Circle Theatre, 1936

Créixer en uns temps difícils maquillats de temps fàcils,
temps amb gent que pateix per mantenir-se, temps
batuts en retirada davant la poca-solta
dels nostres responsables polítics, ha forjat
en mi la complaença a amargar-me, turment
que emana de l'absència de confiança i causa
grans danys.
         A contracor, em condemno a inhibir-me
de les mundanitats socials i ho pal·lio
posant-me en mans d'un "art" compensador.
                     Sóc l'home
"contemplativus," l'home de cultura llibresca
amb sortides plebees, l'home racional,
l'home que no surt gaire perquè no té amb qui fer-ho
o no té companyies que li siguin prou grates
o que baixa al nivell del carrer i es dissol
en l'animació febril i sinergètica
de la riuada humana a l'hora de l'esbarjo
(representacions, compres, àpats, concerts . . .).
És el postpensament i l'utilitarisme
el que ha reemplaçat el pensament i els actes
del ciutadà mitjà que ha sortit a distreure's.
També anomenen fleuma al just, Bildungsroman
al sacrifici, abdomen a la panxa. La base
del seu èxit deu ser la llibertat.
                   Cobertes
les necessitats bàsiques, del meu interior
més estantís sorgeix l'arronsament d'espatlles
que trunca l'obertura als altres i no sé
on fa cap, sostingut, tot jo, pel roig foscant.

The Circle Theatre, 1936

Growing up in a hard time cosmeticized as an easy time,
a time when people sweat blood to support themselves,
a time that beats a retreat before the damn foolishness
of our responsible politicians, has forged
in me an embittered complacency, a torment
that emanates from lack of trust and causes
a lot of damage.
      Unwillingly I'm doomed to shy away
from social worldliness and paper over it
by putting myself in the hands of a compensatory art.

I'm homo contemplativus, a man of bookish culture
with plebeian escapes, a man of reason, a guy
who hardly gets out for he has nobody to get out with,
or no pals sufficiently to his liking,
and who descends to street level, dissolving
in the feverish, synergetic movement
of the human floodtide at leisure
(shows, shopping, meals, concerts . . .).
The postscript and utilitarianism
have taken the place of thought and action
for the average urbanite who seeks diversion.
They characterize a weak will as fairness, the Bildungsroman
as sacrifice, the abdomen as the belly. The basis
of their success must be freedom.
        After covering
the basic necessities, a shrug of the shoulders
bobs up from the stagnation inside me
cutting short any overture to others, and I don't know
where it'll lead, sustained as I am by the red dusk.

Night Windows, 1928

El dret a encendre els llums de l'habitació,
de nit, i a donar un tomb amunt i avall mig nua
sense córrer cortines ni abaixar persianes
i, de pas, a observar-la d'un tros lluny a través
dels finestrals.
                    Les ganes de saber què serà
d'ella d'aquí a molts anys, quan tots siguem "uns altres."

El pretext per quedar-me immòbil rere uns vidres,
no provocar cap canvi ni posar res en ordre.

El greu que sap de "veure" sense poder "saber."
Coneix *L'amant de lady Chatterley*? Va al teatre?
Intenta ser feliç? Pateix depressions?

La traça a imaginar-se-la com una astuta sílfide
estesa amb regust clàssic sobre un fresc sòl claustral,
quasi poetitzada per Pere Serafí.

L'avantatge de ser colpit d'emoció
furtivament i a canvi d'un desengany segur.

L'esforç per sentir fressa on no se sent ni un so,
per percebre tragins en el si del no-res.

El temor de mirar fixament com es miren
corpuscles, aus, satèl·lits, i no obtenir respostes.

La propensió a creure's tot el que es veu quan tot,
per regla general, fa ferum d'impostures.

Night Windows, 1928

The right to switch on the lights in the bedroom
at night and to take a turn back and forth half naked
without drawing curtains or lowering blinds
and, chancing by, to peep at her a little ways away
through the tall windows.
      The desire to know what'll come
of her, years from now, when we all turn into "someone else."

The lame excuse of my staying put behind the glass,
not to trigger any change or tidying things up.

The kicker of being able to "see" but unable to "know."
Is she up on *Lady Chatterley's Lover*? Does she go to the theatre?
Mean to be happy? Suffer from depression?

The artfulness of picturing her as some crafty sylph
stretched out in classic bad taste on a cool cloister floor,
as if poeticized by Pere Serafí.

The advantage of tingling with excitement
on the sly in return for a sure letdown.

The strain to hear noise where not a sound can be heard,
to detect commotion in the thinnest of air.

The creepiness of watching unblinkingly the way we watch
corpuscles, birds, satellites—and without getting a response.

The propensity to believe in everything you see when everything,
as a general rule, gives off a whiff of imposture.

House at Dusk, 1935

És nova la meva afició
per Puccini. Menys recent, en canvi,
és la que tinc per Bach o per l'*Ave Maria*
de Schubert. Fa uns quants anys, la meva indiferència
era absoluta. Per dir-ho així,
en aquell temps tant se me'n donava
allò que no-procura-un-plaer-immediat,
allò que no-modela-conductes-i-criteris,
allò que no-segueix-el-diktat-de-la-massa
(com també m'era igual l'amor no correspost,
la fortalesa de les arrels
dels bellaombres o la salut
del cabell). El trànsit per la vida
transforma les motivacions,
els pensaments i les actituds
sota una confusió d'enteses
secretes, ventims i espantamosques.
Fent servir uns mots més clars,
el trànsit per la vida
ens posa al nostre lloc.

Mira't ara. Tan formal, tan "savi,"
tan envaït per sensacions
confuses, tan poc esperitat,
tan d'una peça, ocupo,
ja feta la creixença,
un lloc dins l'Estat del benestar,
un lloc entre els que viuen una vida segura,
un lloc en la quietud del pis
a les finestres del qual m'aboco
per deixar que la vista recorri els edificis
adjacents, el vessant salvat per una escala
i l'ampla zona verda estesa rere seu
mentre es projecten a contrallum
sobre un crepuscle de sofre i llim.

House at Dusk, 1935

My fondness for Puccini
is new. Less recent, on the other hand,
is what I feel for Bach or Schubert's
Ave Maria. For some years my indifference
was absolute. At that time
I was abandoning myself, so to speak,
to what doesn't procure instant gratification,
to what doesn't mould conduct and judgment,
to what doesn't follow the diktat of the masses
(just as unrequited love, the strength
of the roots of the ombu tree or the health
of my hair were all the same
to me). One's transit through life
transforms motivations,
ideas and attitudes
beneath a confusion of secret
agreements, rebuffs and fly-swatters.
To put it in plain English,
the transit through life
puts us in our place.

Now look at you. So serious, so savvy,
so overrun by feelings
of perplexity, so rarely possessed,
so much of a piece, I occupy—
having already cut my eye teeth—
a place in the Welfare State,
a place among citizens who live socially secure,
a place in the peace of my apartment
at the windows of which I lean out
to let my gaze survey the buildings
adjacent, the slope (excluding the stair)
and the broad green belt stretching behind it
as they catch the crosslight
against a sunset of sulphur and mud.

Com aquells que asseguren que no claudicaran
"mentre la veritat resti oculta," jo penso
ser ferm en l'acció de contemplar el crepuscle,
avui que és diumenge, des del pis.
L'enfosquiment del cel dóna al meu habitatge
un aire de clandestinitat
i permet veure l'interior
d'altres finestres il·luminades
de dintre estant amb veïns-corcons,
veïns-òlibes, veïns-bardisses,
veïns-de-pigmentació-bruna,
veïns-amb-brots-d'olivera-als-llavis
o veïns-crits que se'm fan presents
en aurèoles entreteixides
com veritables desconeguts.

La nit s'arrela de mica en mica
i, acostumat per l'experiència
a ser espectador passiu, m'agraden
els elements que, extrínsecs
a mi, la componen. Travessada
per un feix de raigs X,
la nit incipient
s'ofereix als meus ulls
amb un nucli central
de frescors i amoníacs.

Like people who promise they won't back down
while the truth remains concealed, I plan
to stick to the act of watching the sunset
from the apartment today (which is Sunday).
The darkening sky envelops my room
in an air of secrecy
and permits me to see inside
other windows illuminated
from within by nag neighbors,
owl neighbors, hedge neighbors,
neighbors in dark pigment,
neighbors with olive branches in their lips
and shouting neighbors
who appear to me in interlacing haloes
like veritable strangers.

Night gradually settles,
and used to being the passive observer
from experience I like
the elements that compose it,
extrinsic to me. Pierced
by a sheaf of x-rays,
the incipient night
offers itself to my eyes
with a central core,
coolness and ammonia.

August in the City, 1945

S'ha d'aprendre a ballar i a parlar moltes llengües
i a treure's pensaments del cap. S'ha de tenir
una manera de comportar-se
anticonvencional i boja.
S'han de radicalitzar els programes
amb els anys. S'han de voler dos fills.
S'ha de passar la realitat
pel sedàs d'una visió lúcida
o, en el pitjor dels casos,
optimista. Cal riure's
d'un mateix i dels altres.
S'ha d'arribar a temps a tot arreu.
S'ha de mirar de fit a fit a l'objectiu
en una franja horària de màxima audiència.
S'ha de romandre als llocs on bat el sol de ple
i exposar-se a un cop d'aire calent i a una bravada
irrespirable i gràvida d'asfalt, pol·lució
imantada i resina, que ossos i pell s'impregnin
de la calda que abrusa els carrers despoblats,
que s'enganxi la roba d'estiu al cos. Després
de mesos de feina exhauridora,
s'han de fer vacances a l'instant.

August in the City, 1945

You've got to learn how to dance and speak lots of languages
and pull ideas out of your hat. You've got to have
a way of comporting yourself
that's nonconformist and nuts.
You've got to radicalize the programs
over the years. You've got to want two kids.
You've got to pass the world
through the sieve of a clear vision
or, when the chips are down,
be an optimist. Got to laugh
at yourself as well as the other guy.
You've got to arrive on time anyoldwhere.
You've got to adjust the lens
with a prime-time audience in mind.
You've got to stay put in spots where the sun blazes
and expose yourself to a blast of hot air and a heavy,
unbreathable stench of asphalt, sticky pollution
and grease, until your skin and bones are steeped
in the heat that sears the deserted streets
and glues your summer clothes to your body. After
months of draining work,
you've got to take that vacation. Presto.

Hotel Room, 1931

A l'hotel hi ha una dona en roba interior
que consulta un horari de trens. Una hora més
i, amb un estat d'ànim abatut
i físicament cama-segada,
farà voltes en cercle per l'habitació
deixant una fragància afruitada en un aire
que desprèn pudor de resclosit.
Una setmana més i no hi haurà seqüeles
palpables. Un any més i entomarà carícies.
Quatre anys més i no hi haurà amanyacs.
Deu anys més i la relació
joventut-vellesa farà figa.
Vint anys més i s'enganxarà a l'"ètica"
expansiva del desmenjament
i d'*El triomf de la voluntat*.
D'aquí a cent anys no hi haurà ningú
que recordi res d'ella.
En dos segles no hi haurà casquets
polars. Transcorreguts
cinc mil milions d'anys,
no quedarà ni el sol.

Hotel Room, 1931

At the hotel a woman in her underwear
pores over a train timetable. An hour later,
in low spirits and bone-tired,
she'll start to pace around the room
leaving a fruity fragrance in the air
that reeks of mustiness.
A week later there'll be no
tangible results. A year later
she'll be the object of caresses.
Another four and no lullabies.
Another ten and the delicate balance
between youth and age will be gone.
Another twenty and she'll cling
to an expansive ethics of listlessness
and *Triumph of the Will.*
Another century and nobody's
going to remember a thing about her.
In two centuries there'll be
no polar ice caps. When five
billion years go by,
there won't even be a sun.

Morning Sun, 1952

Un bon dia mires fixament
una persona i penses:
aquesta persona té un passat.
En té, sense cap dubte, com també té un futur,
però no distingeixes ni el passat ni el futur
que la componen. L'un, el futur, és un germen
en estat latent i, per això,
no es veu. L'altre, el passat, ha tingut lloc fa temps
i per aquest motiu es dilueix, ocult
pels remolins tergiversadors.

Hi ha una dona jove a casa seva
asseguda sobre el llit que mira
a través de la finestra. El sol,
de tan fort que és, inflama l'exterior i forneix
de llum natural el dormitori,
llum llevantina que s'apodera
de qualsevol angle com la lava.
A vegades, com tretes de sota terra, esberles
del món d'abans li pugen al pensament i fan
un sobreesforç per revenir,
prova inconcussa d'un viure previ,
no cicatritzat del tot, reclòs
dins una cota de malla a fi
de fer possible l'expansió
d'un viure posseït per un nou intel·lecte.

Sap que segueix un ordre i que fa el que ha de fer.
Sense passos enrere i passos endavant,
sense caigudes i revifades,
seríem invisibles
com la ira o els records.
No m'hi va ni m'hi ve
però trobo que sí,
que s'ha de seguir un ordre
i no badar ni un pèl.

Morning Sun, 1952

One fine day you fix your eyes
on someone and think:
this person has a past.
She has, without doubt, just as she has a future,
but you can't discern the past or future
that make her up. The future is a germ
in its latent state and for this reason
can't be seen. The past took place long ago
and for this reason is diluted, hidden
by distorting whirlpools.

A young woman is at home
sitting up in bed, looking
out the window. The sun,
strong as it is, sets ablaze the exterior
furnishing the bedroom with natural light,
levantine light, which takes possession
of every corner like lava.
At times, as if extracted from underground,
fragments of the previous world well up
into her mind and strive to return,
unshakable proof of a former life,
not completely scarred over,
sheathed in a coat of mail
to enable the germination
of a life possessed by a new intellect.

She knows she follows some order
and does what she has to do.
Without steps backward and forward,
without setbacks and comebacks,
we'd be invisible
like anger or memories.
To me it's neither here nor there
but yes, I do find
you have to follow some order
and not daydream one iota.

Summertime, 1943

La noia de la casa de l'escala de pedra
ha sortit al carrer
balancejant el cos
com fa cada matí.
Ho saps? Saps per què em vénen
aquestes ganes boges
de posar sobre seu
els meus ulls desvetllats?
Saps per què perdo l'esma
quan la veig que s'atura
a encarar-se amb la llum
de l'estiu? O per què
apareix als meus somnis
entre blanques petúnies?
A la meva manera,
el fet de resseguir
la noia de la casa de l'escala de pedra
laboriosament
amb la mirada em salva:
1. De matar les hores buscant de cua d'ull
pel mig de la ciutat abrasada pel sol
persones que són cors de carxofa o problemes,
noies esgrogueint-se al mateix temps que el viure,
un clown amb maletí o uns obrers que s'esllomen
lluny de Pirró, de Gòrgies i d'aquells que proclamen:
"La presa del poder pel proletariat
mena a perpetuar el poder que, corrupte,
passa a altres mans i prou!" alçant la veu en va.
2. De trencar els lligams entre la meva psique
i la realitat, difícils totes dues.
Llavors m'inhibiria, com un tòtil, del món,
vegetaria al marge dels plaers de la vida
i em quedaria inert mentre d'altres es treuen
de damunt l'acritud a força d'observar
la noia de la casa
de l'escala de pedra.

Summertime, 1943

The girl from the house with the stone stoop
has gone out into the street
swaying her body
just as she does every morning.
You know what? You know why they come to me
these crazy desires
to rest on her
my insomniac eyes?
You know why I lose my north
when I see her pull up
to come face to face with the summer
light? Or why she appears
in my dreams
among white petunias?
The act of checking out
the girl from the house with the stone stoop
painstakingly
is my way of sparing myself:
1. From killing time, searching out the corner
of my eye through half the sun-blasted city
for people who are artichoke hearts or creeps,
girls who turn pale along with their lives,
some clown with a briefcase or dog-tired workers
far from Pyrrho, Gorgias and those who proclaim,
"The seizure of power by the proletariat
leads to perpetuating that power which, corrupted,
passes to other hands and that's all she wrote!"
raising their voices in vain.
2. From cutting ties between my psyche
and reality, both of them a hard business.
If that happened, I'd shy away from the world
like a toad, vegan on the fringe of life's pleasures,
passive while others rid themselves of acrimony
by dint of watching
the girl from the house
with the stone stoop.

3. D'acabar esbrinant que estic en un engany,
que la vida sencera és una gran mentida,
que les frustracions, els moments reeixits,
els intents de sortir del pas o fins i tot
la noia de la casa
de l'escala de pedra
no tenen en el fons cap fonament real.

3. From finally realizing that I'm deluded,
that my whole life is a cock-and-bull story,
that the frustrations, right moments,
attempts to get out of a tight spot
and even the girl from the house
with the stone stoop
fundamentally lack any real foundation.

Nighthawks, 1942

(No és el local clàssic sol·licitat pels turistes que van a la caça d'emocions. No és l'establiment on trobareu famosos recolzats al taulell xerrant amb el cambrer o el propietari. No és el lloc de reunió d'intel·lectuals i artistes que fatxendegen entre copes i núvols de fum. No és el bar amb una clientela formada per joves galtaplens que agafen forces per prosseguir la seva interminable ruta nocturna. Es tracta, simplement, d'un humil cafè amb façanes de vidre rere els quals s'arreceren quatre gats a mitjanit mentre tot de penombres dominen els carrers, un cau d'"aus nocturnes" on els comptats noctàmbuls es floreixen. Avui, per exemple, tenim asseguts a la barra un home esprimatxat amb tern i barret de feltre i, amb ell, una dona escardalenca de cabell d'un color de caoba rogenc ben pentinat que llueix un vestit que també tira a roig. Es pot donar per segur que ell la desitja, però és un home massa indecís.)

HOME: Segurament ho duc escrit als ulls.

DONA: Ja ho crec.

HOME: De debò que transmeto males vibracions?

DONA: El cas és que transmets tensió i malestar.

HOME *(agafa aire)*: No en tenia ni idea.

DONA: Deixa-ho córrer.

HOME: He tingut
uns dies impossibles
i pateixo per tot.

DONA: Si no pots fer-hi més,
mira de no pensar-hi.

HOME: Sona molt bé però . . .

DONA: I què en treus, de pensar-hi?

HOME *(després d'una pausa)*: Vols prendre res més?

DONA: Vinga.

HOME *(amb resolució al cambrer)*: Porti'ns una altra ronda.

CAMBRER: De seguida.

HOME *(a la dona)*: M'hi jugo el que vulguis que encerto
el que penses. També llegeixo el pensament.

DONA *(fa un somriure)*: No en tens ni la més mínima idea del que penso.

HOME: És molt fàcil saber-ho perquè ho portem escrit
als ulls. Miro els teus ulls i sé tot el que penses.

Nighthawks, 1942

(It isn't a classic spot sought by tourists who go cruising for thrills. Nor an establishment where you'll find celebrities, elbow on the counter, chatting with a waiter or the owner. Nor a haunt of intellectuals and artists who posture amid drinks and clouds of smoke. Nor a bar with a clientele of fat-cheeked young guys fortifying themselves before pursuing their interminable nightly routine. It is simply a modest café with plate-glass windows behind which a few strays take shelter around midnight while myriad shadows command the streets, a nest of night birds where the occasional noctambulist efforesces. Tonight, for example, we have seated at the counter a slender man in a felt hat wearing a three-piece suit and beside him a skinny woman with neatly combed hair the reddish color of mahogany, sporting a dress that is also a shade of red. You can take it for granted that he desires her, but he is an overly indecisive man.)

Man: I've sure got it written in my eyes.
Woman: You bet.
Man: Am I really sending out the wrong signals?
Woman: Fact is, you seem jumpy, in a stew.
Man (*taking a deep breath*): I had no idea.
Woman: Let's drop it.
Man: I've had
   some lousy days
   and I agonize over everything.
Woman: If that's all you can do,
   try not to think about it.
Man: That sounds just fine, but—
Woman: What did thinking ever get you?
Man (*after a pause*): Want something else?
Woman: I thought you'd never ask.
Man (*resolved, to the waiter*): Give us another round.
Waiter: Right away.
Man (*to the woman*): I'll bet you whatever you want
   I can guess what you're thinking. I read minds too.
Woman (*smiling*): You don't have the faintest idea of what I'm thinking.
Man: It's a snap because we wear it written in our eyes.
   I can look in yours and know everything.

DONA: Se me'n fum el que diguis perquè no pots saber-ho.

HOME: Prou que puc demostrar-t'ho si te'm poses de cara.

DONA: Si es pot saber, quina una se suposa que en porto
   de cap?

HOME: El teu problema és haver descobert
   que a la feina no hi ha ningú insubstituïble,
   que tot és relatiu, que tot és transitori.

DONA: Per què estàs tan segur que és aquest, el problema?

HOME: O potser el teu problema és haver descobert
   que a la vida no hi ha ningú insubstituïble?
   Veig que em guaites i xxxt, solemnement fas mutis.

DONA: Els tràngols hi rebroten, a la feina, a la vida . . .

HOME: Em penso que no passes pel teu millor moment.

DONA (*arqueja les celles*): No hi vull entrar. A les nits
   dormo amb un son feixuc.

HOME (*fent-se'n càrrec*): Hauríem d'animar-nos
   una mica.

DONA: Tots dos estem molt susceptibles.

HOME: Tal com jo ho veig, n'estem.

DONA: I amoïnats i tensos.

HOME: Tens tota la raó.

DONA: La feina és problemàtica,
   i la vida, tres quarts
   del mateix.

HOME: Ben segur.

DONA: Mirem de no pensar-hi.

HOME: Entesos. No hi fa res.

Woman: I don't give a damn what you say: you can't know.

Man: OK. I'll show you if you sit across from me.

Woman: So what do you suppose I've got on my mind?

Man: Your problem is you've realized
   no one at work is irreplaceable,
   everything is relative, everything is temporary.

Woman: How can you be so sure that's the problem?

Man: Or maybe your problem is you've realized
   nothing in life is irreplaceable?
   You've got me in your sights but you just button up.

Woman: The rough patches always come back, at work, in life . . .

Man: I'm thinking this isn't the best time for you.

Woman (*raising her eyebrows*): I don't want to get into it. At night
   I sleep like a top.

Man (*realizing*): We've got to cheer up
   a little.

Woman: We're both very touchy.

Man: Yeah, I've picked up on it.

Woman: And tense and anxious.

Man: We've got good reason to be.

Woman: Work is a problem,
   and life, more or less
   the same.

Man: That's for sure.

Woman: Let's try not to think about it.

Man: Right. It don't matter.

Summer in the City, 1949

L'home buscava riscos,
emocions, plaers de gran calibre, llocs
no folklòrics, negocis,
aproximacions calculades, objectes
del desig que acaparin
l'atenció i conservin
la calma, nous estímuls
frec a frec, indulgències,
encaterinaments, icones sexuals,
proves irrefutables, aventures, consells
posats entre parèntesis, llums verdes, calçat còmode,
formes d'expressió d'una supremacia
pressuposada, entrades de franc per al partit,
maneres de passar l'estona temeràries
i febrils, avantatges abans que planys, respostes
amb cara i ulls. La dona, però, buscava amor.

Summer in the City, 1949

The man is looking for trouble,
thrills, sublime ecstasies, places
short on folklore, deals,
calculated approximations, objects
of desire that grab
your attention and keep
your cool, the latest rage
at your fingertips, binges,
infatuations, sexual icons,
irrefutable proofs, joyrides, advice
within parentheses, green lights, comfy shoes,
forms of expression that presuppose
supremacy, free tickets to the game,
ways of killing time that are reckless and frenzied,
the upper hand before bellyaching, answers
as plain as the nose on your face.
The woman, however, is looking for love.

Excursion into Philosophy, 1959

Hi havia una vegada
un home que es cansava de les coses, de coses
que resulten molestes i d'altres que no ho són;
tan bon punt prorrompien ja s'anaven morint,
esdevingudes coses monòtones i exànimes.
Succeïa tothora i sense més ni més,
com un impuls malsà sorgit de dins. Moria,
l'home, amb allò que mor, renaixia amb les coses
que neixen i moria de nou així que aquestes
morien.
            Sense anar més lluny, s'atabalava
amb l'amor, que envellia corrents, i també amb l'odi
o el menyspreu, tan efímers.
No podia sofrir la fal·libilitat
que ens sotmet, la fatiga
postcoital ni els perquès
de la vida a la Terra
i n'estava ben tip
de Plató i Aristòtil,
de Zenó i Epicur.
Correcta des d'un punt de vista antropològic,
l'autorepressió
dels instints l'embafava
i sentia un enuig
quan corrien bons aires
o es girava la truita.

Amb el coll estrenyent-se per la mandra dels gestos
entre quatre parets,
l'home es fastiguejava
del seu propi desfici.

Excursion into Philosophy, 1959

Once upon a time a man grew weary of things,
things that prove to be irksome and others that don't.
As soon as they came into sight, they started to die,
having turned into monotonous, inanimate things.
It happened all the time and for no particular reason,
like a morbid impulse sprung from within.
The man died, with what dies, was reborn with things
that were born, and died again no sooner than they
died.
        To cut to the chase, he got confused
with love, which aged fast, and hate as well
or disdain, so ephemeral.
He couldn't bear the fallibility
that subdues us, postcoital
fatigue or the whys
of life on Earth
and he wasn't fed up enough
with Plato and Aristotle,
Zeno and Epicurus.
Correct from an anthropological point of view,
self-repression
of the instincts was cloying to him
and he felt annoyed
when things were looking up
or the tables were turned.

His throat constricted by lazy gestures
between four walls,
the man was disgusted
with his own torment.

New York Movie, 1939

Vinc de la ciutat-rebombori i caic
daltabaix del cinema-abisme. El símbol
de la inactivitat és una tarda
a l'enfosquida sala de cinema.
La misantròpica reclusió
en un avenc vistós però irreal.
L'anonimat que ens transfigura en ombres.
La solitud que es deixa embolcallar
dins la projecció de la pel·lícula.
El temps que és esmerçat sense profit
com si la vida durés sempre. En suma:
a fora la metròpoli embogeix
mentre aquí dintre ens abaltim fins tard.

Però eludir les-coses-tal-com-són
té una eficàcia de quatre dies.

N'hi ha que farien el viatge invers.
Cansat, aparto els ulls de la pantalla
i els fixo sobre l'acomodadora
que, dreta al peu de l'escala que puja
a l'exterior, sembla pensativa.
Jove, centrada i de vint-i-un botó,
s'abstreu mentre espera que arribi l'hora
d'aixecar el vol d'aquest cinema infecte
per saltar al coll de la lluent ciutat.

Com ella, el mateix fem també nosaltres,
impenetrables i contradictoris:
encadenar raons amb desraons,
ramificar-nos com camins o rius
i, escindits entre el propi i l'aliè
o el real i el fictici, transitar
incessantment.

New York Movie, 1939

I leave the city-hubbub and fall
head first into the cinema-abyss.
The symbol of idleness is an afternoon
in a pitch-dark movie theater.
Misanthropic seclusion
in a pit alluring but unreal.
Facelessness mutating into shadows.
Enveloping solitude
during the screening.
Time spent to no purpose
as if life lasted forever.
In short: outside the metropolis rages
while inside we doze till late.

Yet things-as-they-are cannot
be dodged for very long.

Some take the opposite route.
Tired, I turn my eyes from the screen
and fix them on the usherette
who, standing at the foot of a stair
that leads to the exit, seems pensive.
Young, focused, in her Sunday best,
she is lost in thought, awaiting the time
she can escape from this corrupt cinema
and fly into the arms of the shining city.

Like her, we do the same,
impenetrable and contradictory:
linking reason to unreason,
dividing ourselves like paths or rivers
and, split between self and other
or real and fictive, in transit
incessantly.

Immersos en el clos
més recòndit dels nostres pensaments,
no ens adonem que el món és poc angèlic,
ni sabem de la vida la meitat.

Plunged in the innermost
recess of our thoughts, we don't
notice the world isn't very angelic,
nor do we even know the half of it.

Girlie Show, 1941

És portentosa la traça que té
la bellesa per fer-nos tornar bojos.
Ens fa perdre el control, interfereix
en la nostra fugida als mars del Sud,
tira per terra els rams de flors, l'honor
i el *Tractatus logico-philosophicus*
i pertorba el desenvolupament
del programa d'activitats diàries.
Ens ocorre amb un quadre (*Girlie Show*,
posem per cas), amb un poema (aquest . . . ?),
amb els celatges atrevits del vespre
o amb una mènada pèl-roja i jove
que, davant una colla de silens,
sàtirs i faunes que fumen i beuen
i amb l'audaç Dionís ficat al cap,
va despullant-se al compàs d'una música.

Ara bé, més traçuda és la lletjor
des que va aprendre, aquesta sí que és bona,
a entrar-nos per l'ull dret transfigurada
en filigrana, guarnida amb agulles
de pit o brins de seda o disfressant-se
amb la simbologia i el decòrum
de la bellesa. I tant! Són les tenebres
que es fan passar per una llum tan casta
com un anyell. És la vulgaritat
que s'uneix a nosaltres per un nexe
de complicitats. És la demagògia
que es fa patent com una panacea.
Són les rates que tenen cara d'àngel.
Serà la mènada pèl-roja i jove
que, davant una colla de silens,
sàtirs i faunes que fumen i beuen
i amb l'audaç Dionís ficat al cap,
va despullant-se al compàs d'una música?

Girlie Show, 1941

Wondrous strange is the skill that possesses
the beauty to drive us out of our minds.
It makes us lose composure, interferes
with our getaway to the South Seas,
flings down sprays of flowers, honor
and the *Tractatus Logico-Philosophicus*
and plays havoc with the unfolding
of the daily program of activities.
It happens with a painting (*Girlie Show*,
for instance), with a poem (the present one?),
with bold mottled clouds in the evening sky
or with a young red-headed votress
who, before a gaggle of centaurs,
satyrs and fauns smoking and drinking,
their minds set on daring Dionysus,
is dancing a striptease in time to a band.

Yet more ingenious still is ugliness
since it came to learn (a boon in itself)
how to enter directly through our eye
transfigured into filigree, adorned
with breast pins and silk laces
or disguised in the symbology and decorum
of beauty. Indeed! It is gloom
made to pass for light as chaste
as a lamb. It is downright vulgarity
binding us to each other by a nexus
of complicities. It is demagoguery
presenting itself as a panacea. It is
the rat that wears the face of an angel.
Can it be the young red-headed votress
who, before a gaggle of centaurs,
satyrs and fauns smoking and drinking,
their minds set on daring Dionysus,
is dancing a striptease in time to a band?

Sunlight in a Cafeteria, 1958

Es veu amb una sola ullada
que és la dona-d'un-altre. Abstreta,
qui sap si neguitosa pel retard
d'algú (l'"altre"?), se sent al mateix temps
a sopluig i perduda, regracia
el meu interès fent-me un cas
com un cabàs i és un hisop
de mira'm i no em toquis. De segur
que no vindria cap a mi
ni amb la saó que dóna un infortuni
(per què hauria de fer-ho si té l'altre?)
ni se m'atansaria com temptada
per l'estuf de ser Déu o impetuosa
com un vent venjatiu. Al capdavall,
de què em serveixen les il·lusions,
o les punyides del desig,
o una dona-del-tot-inassolible
esperant algú en un cafè?

Perquè no tinc a qui esperar,
dono cops d'ull pertot arreu
(al carrer o a la dona de què parlo)
i em distrec amb tot tipus de cabòries.
Un oceà s'estén entre nosaltres.

Sunlight in a Cafeteria, 1958

A single glance is enough to make you see
she's some other guy's wife. Preoccupied,
maybe worried by somebody's lateness
(the "other guy"?), feeling herself at once
protected and lost, she appreciates
my interest by not giving me the time
of day in a big way. She's a hyssop
to be looked at but not touched. You can bet
she wouldn't ever come over to me,
not even if time should deal her a bad hand
(why would she if she's got the other guy?).
Nor would she sidle up as if tempted
by the vanity to be God or impetuous
like a vengeful wind. When all is said and done,
what can wishful thinking do for me,
or the pricks of desire,
or an altogether unattainable woman
waiting for somebody in a café?

Because I don't have anyone to expect,
I shoot glances every which way
(across the street, at the woman I'm trying to figure)
and get sidetracked by a load of worries.
An ocean lies gaping between us.

Office at Night, 1940

S'han quedat sols, de nit, a l'oficina,
i l'estat de tensió
en què es troben els sumeix
en la incertesa. El despatx
és el seu hàbitat, el succedani
de les seves cases. Forces
suprapersonals constrenyen
l'un i l'altre (d'això se'n diu fer l'orni).
Sense cap mena de dubte,
l'encongiment està arrelat en ells.
Quan pleguen, els neguits es fan menys vius,
i al cap d'un temps s'obliden (Deo gratias).
"Gents privades" penant en "llocs privats"
o, més que en llocs, en una lloriguera
de parets blanques i mobiliari
funcional. Torbat davant la idea
d'un cel nocturn farcit d'estrelles, l'home,
l'home individualitzat i sol,
s'arrapa al malendreç de l'escriptori.
Dreta, la dona busca documents
o vés-a-saber-què a l'arxivador.
Sí, sí, la dona els somnis de la qual
i els escrúpols de l'home convergeixen
en un crònic fracàs. L'ansietat
la va envaint fins que perd
tots els punts de referència.

És el cercle tancat per on s'enfonsen
del retraïment espiritual
a la solitud física, absoluta.

Office at Night, 1940

They stayed at the office, at night, alone,
and the tense atmosphere
wherein they find themselves plunges them
into uncertainty. The workplace
is their habitat, the substitute
for their homes. Forces
suprapersonal constrain
them both (this is called not letting on).
Beyond the slightest doubt,
shyness has taken root in them.
After knocking off, their cares are less intense
and before long forgotten (Deo gratias).
Private people suffering in private places
or, better than places, in a warren
of white walls and functional furniture.
Disturbed when confronting the idea
of a night sky filled with stars, the man,
the atomized and lonely man,
clings to the messiness of his desk.
The woman, standing at the file cabinet,
fishes for documents or something-or-other.
Sure enough, said woman's dreams
and the man's scruples converge
in a chronic fiasco. Anxiety
invades her till she loses
every point of reference.

This is the closed circle
through which they sink
from spiritual withdrawal
to absolute, physical solitude.

New York Restaurant, c. 1922

Faig tres àpats al dia,
vint-i-un a la setmana,
prop de noranta al mes
i mil noranta-cinc
a l'any i, per un cop
que et tinc a taula, no anem gaire a l'hora
i ens avorrim. S'aixequen
de sobte i plenes d'indecisió
les nostres veus per damunt del murmuri
incongruent del local i, després,
com la cosa més natural del món,
torna el silenci entre nosaltres. Alço
la vista, et miro, et dedico algun riure,
mastego de pressa i abaixo els ulls.
Inspecciono els bastonets de pa,
les setrilleres, els coberts, els gots,
els plats, les ampolles. Com si estiguéssim
sota l'efecte d'un calmant, comptem
fins a deu abans d'encetar nous temes,
de demostrar-nos de què som capaços
o d'indicar al cambrer
que ens porti aigua.
                   L'anàlisi
dels fets demostra que l'elecció
de la persona en la qual diposites
les esperances de compenetrar-t'hi
descansa sobre uns fonaments tan dèbils
i està subjecta a un rosari tan gran
d'imponderables que no correspon
sovint a allò que n'esperaves.
                  Torno
a atreure el cambrer cap a mi i tu em dius
que freni, que és assumible l'espera.

New York Restaurant, c. 1922

I eat three meals a day,
twenty-one per week,
about ninety a month
and a thousand-and-ninety-five
in a year, and the one time
I get you to a table, we're out of synch
and bored. Our voices
fraught with indecision suddenly
rise above the ill-matched
murmur in the place and afterwards,
like the most natural thing in the world,
silence returns between us. I lift
my face, look at you, flash you a smile,
mumble hastily and lower my eyes.
They inspect the breadsticks,
cruets, cutlery, glasses,
plates, bottles. As if we were
under the effect of a sedative, we count
to ten before broaching new topics
or showing what we're up for
or gesturing to the waiter
to bring us water.
                    Analysis
of the data demonstrates the choice
of the person in whom you place
the hope of sharing your feelings
rests on a pretty flimsy foundation
and is subject to an endless rosary
of imponderables that often don't
correspond to what you hoped.
                            I turn
to catch the waiter's eye but you tell me
don't, we can deal with the wait.

New York Office, 1962

Si us plau, si us plau, que no ho hàgim pensat
fins ara no vol dir que no existeixi.

Perquè existeix. És com una impotència
o un descoratjament que inhabilita
per sortir del-fons-d'on-estem. Com fer-nos-ho
per ser al bell principi de tot? Com fer-nos-ho
per "posar-se en contacte" amb la persona
que més t'interessaria conèixer?

La voracitat empresarial
ens va corrompre el caràcter. Calia
buscar noves relacions pragmàtiques
entre els treballadors, l'economia
i l'Estat i al final vam agafar
una espècie de complex de culpa
perquè no hi ha qui faci un pas i et quedes
amb el dubte de si en un món que viu
de les aparences es pot no creure
allò que et diuen, no prendre un mal gest
o arribar a pensar que aguantem el xàfec.
Ara el que vols és ser tot seu, i t'honra.
Et lliures a la tasca de pretendre-la,
de donar-li un amor que a aquells que es tenen
només a si mateixos els faria
delir, d'oferir-li una convivència
sense compassos d'espera. Elegant,
alta, rossa i amb una agraciada
constitució física, la mires
com en un gag de pel·lícula muda,
sense deixar de perfeccionar-te
i eludint el contacte visual
quan passes de llarg pel davant del lloc

New York Office, 1962

Please, please, if we didn't think of it
till now doesn't mean it doesn't exist.

Because it does exist. It's like a weakness
or despondency that disables us
from leaving the rut we're stuck in. What can we do
to be at the very origin of things? What can we do
to put ourselves in touch with the person
we're just dying to get to know?

Entrepreneurial greed
corrupted our character. It was vital
to search for new pragmatic relations
between workers, the economy and the State
but at last we succumbed to a guilt complex
because nobody makes the slightest move
and you're left doubtful whether in a world
that thrives on appearances you can't believe
in what they tell you, can't take a bad turn
or wind up thinking we should grin and bear it.

Now you want to be all hers—to your honor.
You're devoted to the task of courting her,
of giving her a love that would destroy
whoever keeps entirely to themselves,
of offering to make her fast your wife
in nothing flat. Elegant, tall, blond,
she has attractive physical proportions,
and you get a load of her as in a gag
from some silent movie, without neglecting
to spruce yourself up or to shy away
from eye contact whenever you pass the place

on treballa. Envidrada i a peu pla
del carrer, l'oficina te la mostra
com un delicat maniquí de cera.

Seria lògic que tingués sentit
el que fem. Ben al contrari, no en té.

where she works. Encased in glass
at street level, the office exhibits her
to you like a delicate wax mannequin.

This would be logical if what we do
made sense. On the contrary, it doesn't.

Summer Evening, 1947

Ser dos reporta el doble d'alegries.
Ser dos implica el doble de despeses.
Ser dos dobla els afanys de guany i els somnis
frustrats. Ser dos vol dir que una unitat
deixa de ser la cosa indivisible
i única que per sort o per desgràcia
fou anteriorment. Ser dos és fer-se
malbé la vista junts i remenar
la cua i córrer en paral·lel. Ser dos
té el "problema afegit" de no ser quatre.

Ser dos incita a enraonar. Ser dos,
tal com ho sents, llangueix sense converses,
passant gradualment del dinamisme
a l'electrocardiograma fix,
converses com si diguéssim molt simples,
converses suggeridores del zen,
converses amb el radi d'acció
de les xafarderies viscerals,
converses retrobades en el porxo,
converses que arriben a interferir
en les gesticulacions fogoses.

Ser dos deixa un pòsit: és el contagi
emocional entre les persones
que s'estimen que torna concordants
els seus comportaments, els seus impulsos,
els seus estats d'ànim, el que ignoraven
fins aleshores i la consciència
d'haver donat fi a la contenció.

Summer Evening, 1947

Being a couple is twice the fun.
Being a couple is twice the cost.
Being a couple doubles your earning power
and your frustrated dreams.
Being a couple means a unity
stops you from being the indivisible
and unique thing you once were
for better or worse.
Being a couple is ruining your eyesight
together and shaking your booties in synch
and jogging side by side. Being a couple
brings the "added problem" of not being three or four.

Being a couple makes you talk it over. Being a couple,
I've sensed, languishes without conversation,
slipping eventually from the dynamic
to the stable EKG,
conversation that's very simple, so to speak,
conversation evocative of zen,
conversation with the social impact
of visceral gossip,
conversation rediscovered on the porch,
conversation that winds up interfering
with passionate moves.

Being a couple produces side effects:
it's the emotional contagion between people
who love one another, reconciling
their behavior, impulses,
mental states, what they didn't know
up to that point with the awareness
of having put an end to restraint.

Rooms for Tourists, 1945

Quan vas entrar en la meva vida, entrares
no pas silenciosament, sinó
com en aquells imprevistos que et treuen
del conformisme. Tou, sense saber
com resistir-m'hi, vas desfer els grumolls
del meu aguant, esdevingueres l'únic
desideràtum i te'm vas ficar
a dins.
        Després passàrem per diversos
avatars i una selva de troballes,
i et vas fer gran. Vas créixer, de manera
exponencial, fins a omplir l'espai
que em fixa i estendre't pertot arreu.
Tota actuació humana resulta
dubtosa en la seva imperfecció.
Podria enumerar una llarga llista
de motius que em mogueren a un descens
en picat, però aquí ens teniu, tots dos,
aquesta nit sufocant i ociosa
i sota un cel emmantellat d'estrelles,
amb el nostre deambular distès.
La llum dels fanals i els aparadors
ens cau cal·ligrafiada al damunt
com un espargiment d'hemoglobina.
Els noctàmbuls no es tomben a seguir-nos,
ni els perdularis, ni els cotxes patrulla.
Són moments en què sembla immarcescible
la joventut i aquesta es converteix
en el gran factor de prosperitat.

Rooms for Tourists, 1945

When you entered my life, on no account
did you enter quietly, but like
those unexpected things that exclude one
from conformism. Pliable, not knowing
how I might hold out, you dissolved the lumps
of my endurance, became the only
desideratum and got yourself
under my skin.
            Then we passed through varied
avatars and a forest of found objects,
and you got bigger. You grew
exponentially till you filled the space
where I'm fixed and you spread all over.
Every human action turns out to be
dubious in its imperfection.
I could enumerate a long list
of motives that drove me to fall
headlong, but here we are, the two of us,
on this stifling, leisurely night
beneath a sky mantled with stars
as we take our perambulation.
Light from lampposts and storefronts
falls calligraphed upon us
like a sprinkling of hemoglobin.
Nightwalkers don't turn to follow us,
nor lowlifes, nor patrol cars.
These are moments when youth appears
unfading, converted
into the great factor of success.

Western Motel, 1957

Que em vas agradar des del primer dia
ja ho he donat a entendre prou. Tens por
que entrem en l'esfera de l'impossible
quan pretenem crear un "terreny neutral"
per a la comprensió i el respecte
perquè a l'amor, l' ἔρως, li és inherent
la discòrdia i el recel. L'herència
biològica i l'educació
volgué el destí que et fossin favorables.
Ets íntegra per dir el que cal que es digui
i per guardar silenci quan guardar-lo
ve al cas. Asseguda a l'extrem del llit
amb el cos retallant-se tot enterc
contra la vista de la nostra cambra
sobre els tossals del desert, em preguntes
pel meu lleuger optimisme i jo, que sec
en un racó del quadre escenogràfic,
formulo respostes. I així el susdit
amor, l'amor-a-l'altre, sincronitza
la pujada d'adrenalina abans
que els pneumàtics del cotxe giravoltin
sobre la capa de quitrà bullent
cap a una destinació d'ensomni.

Western Motel, 1957

I liked you from the very first day
as I've made clear enough. You're scared stiff
we're entering the sphere of the impossible
when we try to create a "neutral ground"
for understanding and respect
because discord and mistrust are inherent
in love, ἔρως. Fate willed that
biological inheritance and education
would prove auspicious in you.
You're honest to say what must be said
and to keep quiet when to do so
is fitting. Perched on the edge of the bed,
your body a very erect outline
against the view from our room
over the desert ridges, you ask
about my shallow optimism and I,
gruff in a corner of the stage set,
formulate answers. And so the aforesaid
love, love-for-the-other, synchronizes
with the boost of adrenaline before
the car's tires turn
over the layer of boiling tar
heading for some dream-like destination.

Solitude, 1944

Rodo amb ella al volant del meu vehicle
per una carretera secundària
flanquejada de terres de rostoll
i extensions boscoses que esdevenen
un vague cobertor als meus ulls: en dècimes
de segon el rectangle horitzontal
del polsós parabrisa em dóna vistes
que no tinc temps de registrar i que suren
en l'espai infinit fins que s'escolen,
produint una ratxa sibilant,
a banda i banda del capot.
                                    Pletòric
de facultats, recorro aquest trajecte
com si ho hagués fet sempre (centenars
o milers de vegades), engolint
quilòmetres a una velocitat
acceptable i no trobant més que sots
i pedres pel camí quan emergeix
una construcció de planta baixa
d'entremig d'una arbreda atapeïda
que em reclama l'atenció. La casa,
que també mostra senyals d'estar buida,
la veuré escolar-se a la nostra dreta
deixant anar un xisclet enrogallat.

Una mixtura de sensacions
i veus interiors s'arremolina
al meu cervell. Per ofegar el so ronc
del motor, ja tinc música a la ràdio.

Solitude, 1944

With her at the wheel of my car
I'm rolling down a B road
flanked by stubble fields and
wooded stretches becoming a
blurred quilt to my eyes: in tenths
of a second the horizontal oblong
of dusty windshield yields me sights
I don't have time to register, floating
in infinite space until they slip
away producing sibilant gusts
on either side of the hood.
                              In full
possession of my faculties, I cover
this route as if I'd always done it
(hundreds or thousands of times)
swallowing up kilometers at an
acceptable speed without coming across
anything more than holes and stones
by the road when a ground-floor structure
rises in the midst of a compact grove
demanding my attention. The house
shows signs of being empty.
I'll see it slipping past on our right
letting go a hoarse yell.

A mixture of sensations
and inner voices swirls around
my brain. To muffle the raucous sound
of the engine, I put music on the radio.

Four Lane Road, 1956

La consciència adulta del jo,
de la nostra actual identitat,
dels sentiments de joia i solitud,
del que es pot fer i del que a la fi farem
o de la situació del món
és com els sobresalts que els automòbils
produeixen quan solquen el terreny,
com la mala acció d'aprofitar-se
d'aquells que donen proves de feblesa,
com quan ens sentim nus, mancats de fe,
sense comunicació amb els altres,
amb nul·la autoestima, i ingressem
a la realitat asocial
i franciscana on trobarem abric,
com una tempesta d'estiu fent caure
descàrregues elèctriques i pluges
amb un terrabastall que Déu n'hi do,
com el xiscle d'ocell que li arribà
de nit a Wang Wei des del fresc torrent
o com Xantipa, la dona de Sòcrates,
cada cop que estava de mala lluna.

Four Lane Road, 1956

The adult consciousness of the ego,
of our present identity,
of our feelings of joy and solitude,
of what can be done and what we'll finally do
or of the world situation
is like the sudden fright that cars
produce when they plough through a field,
like the dirty deed of taking advantage
of people who show signs of weakness,
like when we feel naked, lacking in faith,
out of contact with others,
our self-esteem nullified, and we enter
a reality asocial
and Franciscan where we find shelter,
like a summer storm that sends down
electrical discharges and rain showers
with such a roar it scares the bejesus out of us,
like the bird's cry that reached Wang Wei
from the spring gorge one night
or like Xantippe, Socrates' wife,
every time she fell into a bad mood.

Route 6, Eastham, 1941

Fa un no res anava a cent vint, vuitanta,
quaranta. Xino-xano, com la llum
del cel quan sesvaeix un vespre, aparco
el cotxe fora de la carretera
i, així que el velocímetre està a zero,
desconnecto el motor, em desentenc
del tauler de control i focalitzo
la mirada en les cases que s'aixequen,
disperses, al davant.
                              Respiro fort
i, immòbil, em concentro en el vilatge
perquè, per alguna raó, transmet
una sensació de déjà vu,
perquè m'ha fet pensar en una altra vida
més suportable, perquè l'associo
amb el record de quan érem més joves
i tornàvem de matinada a casa
per carreteres i carrers deserts
fent tentines sota els fanals, els pins
i la lluna cara-rodona i blanca
com una piloteta de ping-pong.

Deixo d'abandonar-me a uns pensaments
no sé si tranquil·litzadors o inútils.
No cal dir que les coses són com són
i que la resta és fer castells a l'aire.

El dia és lleganyós, hi ha molt poc trànsit
i un silenci abismal. De nou, engego
el motor, premo l'accelerador
a fons i surto disparat d'aquí.

Route 6, Eastham, 1941

Not long ago I was going one twenty,
eighty, forty. Inchmeal, like the light
in the sky when dusk fades, I pull
the car onto the side of the highway
and soon as the speedometer hits zero
I switch off the engine, think no more
about the dashboard and concentrate
my gaze on the scattered houses
that loom up in front.
                         I take a deep breath
and dead still I focus on the village
because for some reason it lets out
a feeling of déjà vu, because
it makes me think of another life,
more bearable, because I associate it
with the memory of when we were younger
and used to come back home at daybreak
down highways and deserted streets
staggering beneath streetlights, pines
and the moon, round-faced and white
like a ping-pong ball.

I reel myself in from thoughts I can't
tell whether they're reassuring or vain.
No need to say that things are as they are
and the rest is building castles in the air.

The day is sleepy, hardly any traffic,
an abysmal silence. Once again
I start the engine, floor the gas
and fishtail out of here.

Gas, 1940

S'aixeca pols en aturar-se el cotxe
ran de la benzinera i l'empleat
que maneja els assortidors no gira
ni els ulls.
        Ben apartat de tot desori,
l'indret és una clariana al cor
d'un bosc sotmès a una obagor feréstega,
el sol que cau l'abriga amb una capa
de llum somorta i, com un viarany
avancívol, la carretera es perd
en un revolt entre els frondosos arbres
que la flanquegen.
        Dels matolls i l'herba
i la terra s'exhalen colpidores
aromes que penetren els pulmons.

El carrisqueig cadenciós dels grills
ressona en l'aire espurnejant del vespre.

Els contorns que es dominen amb la vista
es dissoldran sense tardar com sucre
o pigments vegetals.
        Un cop aquí,
tot fent una parada a mig trajecte,
una gradació de solituds
alça la cara: hi ha la soledat
que bufa amb el vent fluix que mou les fulles
i les branques i aquella que és costosa
d'abordar, hi ha la solitud de l'erm
i la que solament experimenten
els qui s'arrapen al volant del cotxe
i fugen de la solitud urbana
i, lliscant sobre estretes carreteres,
s'aturen on el bosc és més esquiu.

Gas, 1940

Dust rises as the car pulls to a stop
at the filling station and the attendant
who works the pumps doesn't even turn
his eyes.
        Far removed from any commotion,
the spot is a clearing in the heart
of a forest subdued by an uninviting shadiness.
The fading sun wraps it in a cloak
of muted light, and like a fast
track the highway disappears
around a bend between the leafy trees
that flank it.
        Thickets and grass
and earth exhale pungent
scents that penetrate the lungs.

The crickets' cadenced grating echoes
in the luminescent evening air.

The forms our sight encompasses
will dissolve before long like sugar
or vegetable colors.
        Once here,
with everything halted in midcourse,
a gradation of solitudes
lifts its face: the solitude that wafts
with the slack wind stirring leaves
and branches and the kind that costs dearly
to reach, the solitude of wilderness
and the kind experienced only
by those who grip the steering wheel
to escape from urban loneliness
gliding over narrow highways
to stop where the forest is most impenetrable.

Hills, South Truro, 1930

M'he enfilat dalt de tot de la muntanya
per parlar amb mi mateix. Ja saps,
del present, del futur.
                              Assolellant-me,
he tingut la prerrogativa
de veure a venir moltes coses.
Deu ser per les olors de terra
i mar distant que em conhortaven.
Deu ser pels cants d'ocell. Deu ser
pels trens. Deu ser per la grandesa
d'aquestes vistes?
                              Al batent
del sol he deixat córrer la mirada
i he comprès els meus límits i que un cúmul
d'assumptes em destorben. Que em distrec
amb punts de llum exigus. Que consagro
la no-immortalitat al no-fer-res.
Que sento un xiuxiueig a les entranyes.

No dic res i el món que m'envolta
d'improvís em fa seu i se m'enduu.
M'alleugereixo. Em torno foliífer,
i també puc fer flors. M'agrada,
del cim estant, la contemplació
sobrehumana dels dominis.

Però, més tard, em tocarà
baixar a la plana, de retorn
amb els meus, i llavors, com si tal cosa,
tornaré a fer com cada dia,
malbaratant temps i recursos.

Hills, South Truro, 1930

I climbed to the very top of the mountain
to speak to myself. You know,
about the present, the future.
                              Bared to the sun,
I held the prerogative
of seeing many things coming to pass.
It must be due to the scent of earth
and distant sea, which were consoling.
It must be due to birdsong. It must be
due to trains. Is it due to the grandeur
of this vista?
                    As the sun
beat down I allowed my gaze to range
and understood my limits and that a slew
of pot-boilers hinders me. That I am diverted
by punk points of light. That I dedicate
no immortality to doing nothing.
That I hear a whisper from inside.

I utter not a word and the surrounding world
suddenly possesses me and bears me away.
I grow lighter. Become leaf-bearing
and even burst into bloom. From the peak
I delight in the superhuman
contemplation of dominions.

But thereafter my lot will be
to descend to the plain, returning
to my kind, and thus, as if I were such,
I shall resume an everyday likeness
squandering time and resources.

Corn Hill (Truro, Cape Cod), 1930

Bo i recorrent les faldes dels turons
et trobes un pendís darrere l'altre
i pujants que mereixen un respecte.

Et trobes prats plens d'ombra i plens de sol
amb vegetació desespessida
i vida vegetal compacta.
                     Et trobes
cops d'aire remorosos imitant
sense repòs els sons dels esbarzers,
els sospirs o les llaunes de refrescos
i un oratjol que travessa tot net
les senderes.
              Com dos i dos són quatre,
et trobes un entramat de camins
debolits i coberts de males herbes
que formen ondulacions i es corben
en relleus i retombs inacabables
i llargs trams rectes que et porten on vulguis.

Et trobes tamisatges divisoris
entre el vers líric i el discurs comú.

Et trobes una escampada de cases
que s'ensenyoreixen d'un cim pelat
com refugis d'antics anacoretes
on no prendre's la vida a la valenta
i estendre roba més a prop del cel.

Corn Hill (Truro, Cape Cod), 1930

While scouring the hillsides
you discover one slope behind another
and rises that merit a certain respect.

You discover fields full of shade and sun
with sparse vegetation
and compact plant life.
                              You discover
sonorous blasts of air incessantly
imitating sounds of brambles,
sighs or soda cans
and a breeze that sweeps the paths
completely clean.
                         As two plus two make four,
you discover a network of trails
eroded and weed-covered
undulating and curved
into bumps and endless turns and
long straight lines that take you where you want.

You discover the siftings that separate
lyric verse from ordinary discourse.

You discover a spread of houses
that command a barren cliff
like the havens of ancient anchorites
where life isn't lived like there's no tomorrow
and clothes are hung out closer to the sky.

Cape Cod Morning, 1950

De bon matí, s'acostuma a mirar
per la finestra perquè n'adquiríem
l'hàbit i els hàbits adquirits no es perden.
Se sol fer per mera rutina, amb cara
inexpressiva, com quan ens llevem
o ens convertim en un zero a l'esquerra.

De bon matí, s'acostuma a mirar
per la finestra empesos per estímuls
de sobres coneguts: el fresc oreig
procedent dels costers o els pics nocturns
que cala les articulacions
i ens reanima, la llum natural
que es reflecteix damunt la superfície
del pla i el bosc que embolcallen la casa
o el desenfeinament que ens obre els ulls
a les dents de lleó.
                    De bon matí,
s'acostuma a mirar per la finestra
amb la ferma esperança de brindar
un cel tan llis i ardent a les retines
que ens demanem de pas per què el termòmetre
no marca encara uns trenta graus centígrads.

Esbatanats els finestrons, es venç
per uns instants la por a la petitesa.

Cape Cod Morning, 1950

Early in the morning you're used to looking
out the window because we acquired
the habit and habits acquired aren't lost.
You usually act out of mere routine, face
inexpressive, as when we roll out of bed
or turn into a nobody.

Early in the morning you're used to looking
out the window driven by inducements
overly familiar: the balmy zephyr
descending from slopes or nocturnal peaks
seeping into the joints
and reviving us, the natural light
reflected on the surface
of the plain and the woods enwrapping the house
or the disengagement that opens our eyes
to dandelions.
                    Early in the morning
you're used to looking out the window
with the firm hope of offering a toast
to a sky so smooth and burning on the retinas
we wonder in passing why the thermometer
still doesn't read thirty degrees centigrade.

With the shutters open wide, fear
vanquishes pettiness for a moment.

Cape Cod Afternoon, 1936

La predicció meteorològica
era clara: a la tarda augmentaria
una mica la nuvolositat
i es girarien vents més forts. Ocorre
sovint.
       Sense forçar el motor, les tardes
són perfectes per satisfer el desig
d'escriure, metabolitzar els plaers
i flagells del moment i fer projectes
a curt termini.
        El moderat ressol
és una farsa tràgica del disc
solar. La mansuetud catatònica
de les hores és un senyal d'avís
del compte enrere. El desplegament d'ombres
generoses sobre els exteriors
i el terra de la casa és un emblema
de la inexorabilitat dels canvis.

Es viuen diferents vides en una,
indoblegables, singulars, autònomes,
com un flist-flast. Per exemple, la mena
de viure que aquí es comenta respon,
a coll d'aquesta tarda vagarosa,
a la descripció de les tranquil·les.

Cape Cod Afternoon, 1936

The weather forecast was clear:
the afternoon would see
a slight increase in cloudiness
and the wind would turn stronger. A frequent
happenstance.
                        Without pushing it, afternoons
are perfect for satisfying desire
to write, metabolizing pleasures
and scourges of the moment and making
short-term plans.
                        The moderate glare
is a tragic farce of the solar
disk. The catatonic tameness
of the hours is a warning sign
for the countdown. The unfurling of generous
shadows over the house,
its exterior and grounds, is an emblem
of inevitable change.

Every life is the site of different lives—
unbending, singular, autonomous,
in succession, bang-bang.
The kind expounded here, for instance,
on the back of this leisurely afternoon,
answers to the description of quiescence.

Cape Cod Evening, 1939

N'hi ha moltes més, de ganes de fer el mandra,
quan les clarors vesprals desmagnetitzen
els camins i la brossa i el bosquet,
donen al dia un to grisenc i esporguen
arestes i margallons.
                                    Però cal,
que passi això, perquè tots, el marit,
la muller, el gos, s'estiguin en silenci
sense la pressió dels protocols,
sentin el vent xiulant entre les branques
o flairin una olor de figues.
                                    Oh
com vagaregen els seus ulls (mig clucs,
en caure la tarda) pels regalims
de les soques, la brosta, les arrels,
les taques d'ombra, els formiguers, les pedres
i els llangardaixos dels camps del voltant.

Qui més qui menys fa els comptes de les ànimes
d'éssers pròxims que han pres, potser, la forma
de gotes tornassolades de pluja.

Cape Cod Evening, 1939

You really feel like lazing around
when twilight takes the glamour off
the paths, the underbrush and the woods,
giving the day a greyish tint, pruning
ears of corn and palms.
                        This has
to happen for all of them—husband,
wife, dog—to fall silent
with no need for pleasantries,
listening to the wind whistle in the branches
or picking up the scent of figs.
                        And how
their eyes (half-closed, as night falls)
wander over the trickle
down the trunks, buds, roots,
the smudges of shadow, ant hills, stones
and lizards in the fields all around.

Everyone more or less counts the souls
of the dear departed who take the form, perhaps,
of iridescent drops of rain.

Cape Cod Sunset, 1934

És com si l'horitzó sobreeixís,
com si la natura marqués el pas
del dia a la nit detenint el temps,
com si esclatés una bomba d'hidrogen.

Sobrevé la posta del sol i el món
embogeix de perfums primaverals
que amaren l'aire i de colors roents
que s'escampen sobre els antropomòrfics
perfils del bosc agrest i les muntanyes.

Grans propietats rústiques que fan
olor de nou, camins de bona petja,
marrades angostes, albercoquers
en flor, carenes, terrenys de pastura,
torrenteres seques i bruguerars
es revesteixen de llustrosos nimbes
rics d'ocres, ambres, safrans i carmins
que a poc a poc es van esllenegant
en inconnexa disposició.
Segons com hi toca la llum, tremolen
de pura ingravidesa i harmonitzen
amb el blau més pujat del firmament.

Cape Cod Sunset, 1934

It's as if the horizon had overflowed,
as if nature had marked the passage
from day to night by slowing time,
as if a hydrogen bomb had exploded.

The sunset broke loose and the world
went crazy with vernal scents
saturating the air, with burning colors
spreading over the anthropomorphic
outlines of wild woods and mountains.

Huge country estates that give
off a fresh smell, fine hiking trails,
narrow detours, apricot trees
in bloom, crest lines, pasture lands,
dry gullies and heather
are graced with glowing haloes,
rich in ochres, ambers, saffrons and carmines,
gradually losing their shapes
in a disjointed arrangement.
According to how the light falls, they tremble
with pure weightlessness and harmonize
with the most intense blue of the firmament.

Briar Neck, 1912

Erms, solcuits i brunyits per la intempèrie,
els espadats rocosos amb grans gorges
descarnades i guerxos replanells
i formacions vegetals suspeses
i codolars al peu del precipici
davallen fins al mar.
                    Ah el mar! Una àguila
incompatible amb merles i verdums,
una disbauxa de fisonomies
i remors diluint-se en l'arc del cel,
una massa d'anyil centellejant
sota la tamisada llum del sol,
un final de trajecte.
                    Dalt del cingle
un aire franc embriaga els sentits.

Briar Neck, 1912

Barren, sun-baked and glistening
from rough weather, rocky crags with deep
gnawn-away gorges and warped landings
hanging plant growth
and rubble at the base of cliffs
descend as far as the sea.
                              The sea! An eagle
at odds with blackbirds and finches,
a debauchery of countenances
and murmurs fading beneath the arch of the sky,
a mass of indigo gleaming
in the filtered sunlight,
a terminus.
                    On the outcrop
a free wind intoxicates the senses.

Rocky Seashore, 1916–1919

Una vintena de metres per sota,
el rompent exhibeix moviments d'aigües
que assoten la línia costanera
amb onades que van a estavellar-se
teledirigides contra els esculls,
les platjoles d'asprositat detrítica
i els farallons que es drecen, com punys closos,
mar endins. Una persona que hi baixi,
posant-hi cura, serà testimoni
des de la privilegiada base
del roquissar i a un pam dels rulls d'escuma
de perspectives úniques, sedants,
on el més-enllà i la immediatesa,
la totalitat i el no-res, s'adiuen.

Les coses comencen a carburar,
una incommensurable plenitud
fa reviure els sentits de mig a mig
i, per primera vegada a la vida,
s'aspira a l'amor ple i la transcendència.

Rocky Seashore, 1916–1919

Some twenty meters below,
the breaker lays bare the tidal currents
that whip the coastline
with waves remote-controlled
smashing against reefs,
patches of rubble-coarsened beach
and sea-stacks that stand erect, like clenched fists,
offshore. Whoever descends there,
gingerly picking his steps, will bear witness—
from the privileged spot on the rockbed
amidst a mass of foamy curls—
to unique, soothing perspectives
where the hereafter and immediacy,
totality and nothingness correspond.

Things start to move,
an incommensurable plenitude
revives the senses inside out
and for the first time in your life
you aspire to unconditional love
and transcendence.

The Lighthouse at Two Lights, 1929

Situat al cim d'un serral planer,
florit i de difícil arribada
al davant d'una platja arenulosa
jaspiada de dunes i pedrenys,
l'imponent far ens féu, aquell matí,
companyia.
         Les hores de calor
eren inacabables i a nosaltres
ens venien molt bé per prendre el sol
i emmorenir-nos.
         La sorra cremava
i per les fenedures del mar calm
passaven brises i sentors salades.
Després de treure's el minieslip
amb els polzes i els índexs, es va ajeure,
arran meu, amb el tors nu boca avall.
Cabells despentinats, omòplats, natges,
plecs ano-períneo-genitals,
talons i així mateix la pell més fosca
que la meva es mostraren a la vista
com si estiguessin fets per satisfer
un capritx.
         Amb les nostres funcions
vitals reduïdes a no tenir
vergonya de ser lliures, es diria
que érem part integrant de la natura.

La vaig mirar sense contenció
i, abans d'estirar-me de panxa enlaire,
em pessigollejà amb un bell somriure.

The Lighthouse at Two Lights, 1929

Standing atop a flat hill
rife with flowers and hard to get to
in front of a sandy beach
streaked with dunes and rocks,
the imposing lighthouse, that morning,
kept us company.
                          The hours of heat
were endless and it suited us
just fine to take the sun
and turn brown.
                          The sand burned
and through the cracks in the placid sea
wafted salty breezes and scents.
After peeling off her minibriefs
with thumbs and forefingers, she lay
face down, her naked body next to mine.
Mussed hair, shoulder blades, buttocks,
the anogenital folds of the perineum,
heels and, to top it off, skin darker
than mine—the works were on display
as if they'd been made to satisfy
some passing fancy.
                                With our vital
signs reduced to feeling no shame
at our bare essentials, you might say
we were an integral part of nature.

I stared at her without restraint
and before I stretched out belly-up
she tickled me with a sweet smile.

Lighthouse Hill, 1927

Les últimes llums de la tarda
provocaven que el mar irradiés
un espurneig metàl·lic.
                Declinant,
el sol ruixava amb ombres els pendents
esclarissats de la lloma i, al punt
més alt, els volts del far.
                Entre el monticle
i l'aigua, entre el terra i el cel,
tirats al nostre tou de platja,
sense cap impuls sexual
ni més objectiu que complaure'ns,
la vaig cenyir amb el braç (tenia
arena, branquillons i grans
de sal enganxats a la pell
calenta).
          Havíem arribat
a funcionar sobre la premissa
d'unes expectatives raonables
i el costum de no prendre'ns res
com a absolut que és tant com assumir
conjuntament la incongruència
ontològica humana i per això,
fosos en la vastitud de la costa,
teníem molts motius per estimar-nos.

Era palès que el dia s'acabava.
Ens vestírem i vam anar-nos-en
romancejant. Beatus ille . . .

Lighthouse Hill, 1927

The last rays of the afternoon
provoked the sea to radiate
a metallic glitter.
                        Calling it a day,
the sun splashed shadows on the patchy
slopes of the ridge and, at the highest point,
the environs of the lighthouse.
                                Between hillock
and water, land and sky, with us
plopped down on our stretch of beach,
without the slightest sexual urge
or more in mind than enjoying ourselves,
I girded her with my arm (grabbing
sand, twigs and grains of salt
stuck to hot skin).
                        We'd reached the point
of operating on the premise
of some reasonable expectations
and the habit of not taking anything
for granted, which is much the same
as jointly assuming an ontological
human incongruity, and this was why,
fused in the vastness of the coast,
we had many motives to love each other.

It was clear the day was over.
We got dressed and beat it
somewhat bemused. Beatus ille . . .

Rooms by the Sea, 1951

Un picadís de lluminositat
ens envesteix. Ex Oriente lux.
Emblanquidora, se'ns aferra amb força.
Des de dins de la casa es veu el mar
delimitat per portes i finestres.
Avui encara fa més bo que ahir
i el cel és ras, com no n'hi ha d'altre. En casos
així, les habitacions fan goig,
de tan espitregades. Les persones
ja saben que ho són tot i no són res.
Prenen posicions i no les prenen.
Quan els arriba el torn d'entrar en raó,
no els vaga. El temps va teixint una xarxa
d'estones perdudes que resumeixen
aquesta summa nostra de silencis
i soledats on ens refugiem.
Mà-llarg i dat-i-beneït i il·lògic,
el cos humà defuig precipitar-se.
On s'és vist enganyar-s'hi, en l'evident?
Impera una tranquil·litat que crea
addicció com un regal dels déus
i és generosa en la policromia.

Rooms by the Sea, 1951

A shard of luminosity
assails us. Ex Oriente lux.
Brightening, it takes us by force.
From inside the house you can see the ocean
delimited by doors and windows. Today
the weather's even nicer than yesterday
and the sky is clear, like no other. At times
like these, the rooms look great,
so unbuttoned. People already
know they're everything and nothing.
They take positions and don't.
When their turn comes to reason, they don't
go woolgathering. Time weaves a net
of lost moments that sum up
this our summa of silences
and solitudes where we take refuge.
Open-handed, over-and-done-with, illogical,
the human body avoids any rushing around.
Where have you seen anyone deceive himself
in the evident? A calmness reigns, creating
addiction like a gift of the gods,
generous in polychromy.

Sun in an Empty Room, 1963

En aquest dormitori buit de mobles
i impol·lut se situa l'acció.
S'ha omplert del raig de sol que deixa entrar
la finestra i els passos dels meus peus
ressonen com si algú vingués amb mi.
Vaig amb l'esquena dreta i amb els ulls
atents a alguna cosa (tant se val,
és clar, a què). Flotant en la claror
nupcial de la tarda (ja vespreja)
he notat la presència d'una ombra,
un batec, un respir. Sóc jo mateix
que, tendint a la invisibilitat,
em retrobo i d'això en deixo constància.

La nuesa d'aquest espai, oberta
en canal per la llum que ve entonada
de fora, és la nuesa de la vida.

És estranya, la vida. Si l'haguéssiu
vista abans, amb les teies del desig
tants cops enceses i les esperances
i els somnis i les satisfaccions
i els clarobscurs de gent engrescadora . . .
Després i sense a penes adonar-te'n
la vida encalla enmig de les sordeses,
els alts i baixos, la monotonia.
De sobte, et desallotgen, o te'n vas,
i la nova mestressa és la buidor.

Amb tot, jo no vaig allunyar-me gaire.
Arreu on vagis, mai no s'ha trobat
la porta de sortida al laberint.

Sun in an Empty Room, 1963

In this bedroom devoid of furniture
and unpolluted the action is set.
It is filled with sunlight admitted
by the window and my footsteps resound
as if someone were walking with me.
I stand up straight, my eyes intent
on something (on what is clearly
unimportant). Floating in the nuptial
glow of afternoon (sun already waning)
I noted the presence of a shadow,
a pulse, a breath. It's just me:
tending to be invisible,
I rediscover myself and leave a sign.

The bareness of this space, cut straight
down by the light that comes delineated
from outside, is the bareness of life.

Which is strange. If you saw it before,
with the torches of desire ablaze
so many times, the hopes
and dreams, the satisfactions
and chiaroscuro of captivating people . . .
Later, without your noticing the pain,
life gets bogged down by deaf ears,
the highs and lows, monotony.
Suddenly they evict you, or you leave,
and the new landlady is emptiness.

All the same, I'm not moving very far.
No matter where you go, you never find
the way out of the labyrinth.

Sea Watchers, 1952

Una vegada s'ha sobreviscut
a les destrosses del capitalisme
avançat i a un mateix, una vegada
ho hem vist i ho hem fet tot, què ens queda, doncs,
sinó l'epifania del balanç?
Per no parlar de la pau d'esperit.
Per no parlar dels records que s'escapen
a la quinta forca, si bé tant és,
perquè el que ens segueix diuen que és més agre.
Per no parlar dels nostres encreuats
destins.
      Segons seriosos estudis
d'impacte ambiental, el que rebem
és el que solc a solc s'ha anat sembrant
però tu i jo no vam sembrar mai res
i exhibim l'alegria d'estar junts
i coneixem la veritat completa
del que hem vist i el que hem fet que a fi de comptes
no consisteix més que en una retícula
de vaguetats, moments i circumstàncies
que no desapareixerà d'escena.
Hi ha hagut un salt qualitatiu en forma
de peces de llenç de blavor ondulant
i llits i oliverars. Tota parella
de banyistes és en aquest context
plausible. Ho saps prou bé. Descrivim òrbites
entorn d'un microcosmos d'alt valor
paisatgístic compost de pols orgànica
i acceptem amb calma que el pas dels anys
ens faci tornar diferents del que érem
i doti de sentit el que era buit
i llevi el sentit del que ja en tenia.
I, mentre la salut ens ho permeti,
contemplarem horitzons de futur
ben bé com si Simeó, l'Estilita,
marqués la nostra manera d'obrar.

Sea Watchers, 1952

Once you've managed to survive
the devastation of late capitalism
as well as yourself, once we've seen
and done it all, what's left for us
but the epiphany of how things stack up?
Not to mention spiritual peace.
Not to mention memories that skedaddle
to the back of beyond, but never mind,
since what follows, they say, stinks even more.
Not to mention our crossed destinies.

According to reputable studies
of environmental impact, what we reap
is what we've been sowing row by row
but you and I have never sown a thing
and we display the joy of being together,
understanding the whole truth of what
we've seen and done which, when tallied,
consists of nothing more than a net
of vague things, moments, situations
which won't disappear from the stage.
A qualitative leap occurred in the form
of an undulating blue piece of canvas
and beds and olive groves. In this context,
every conjugal pair of bathers is plausible.
You've got this down pat. We sketch orbits
around a highly valued microcosm,
a landscape composed of organic dust,
and calmly accept that the march of time
will make us different from what we were,
filling with meaning what was empty
emptying of meaning what contained it.
As long as our health permits,
we'll scrutinize the horizon of the future
as if Simeon the Stylite had stamped
his name on our way of working.

Two Comedians, 1965

El seu final revelà la lleialtat
que van professar-se i l'oxidació
de les cèl·lules i les patologies
més imprevisibles i els plecs d'una pell
que ha anat clivellant-se com la terra seca.
Per tal de ser amb l'altre i que a l'altre també
li vinguessin ganes de ser-hi i de rompre
barreres i de fer fàcil el difícil
i de trobar-se atractius i perspicaços,
per tal en definitiva de complaure's
s'havien reconegut mútuament
des d'una naturalesa que s'inclina
cap a l'ordre i la racionalitat
moderna i havien canviat de gustos
i havien fet ús del sentit de l'humor
per poder-se riure d'un moment històric
proveït de "consciència civil"
i de "tot allò que el públic sol·licita"
i d'"enormes oportunitats perdudes."
No n'hi ha un pam de net. Cloc-pius però impertèrrits,
desmilloradíssims però somrients,
tingueren, en equilibri amb ells mateixos,
el do sempre de la farsa.
                         Ensarronar
és l'autèntic art, la fórmula perfecta
per exhortar els fills-de-sa-mare a aplaudir-te.
Quan en una ocasió van preguntar-los
per les coses en què creien van respondre
que en aquelles coses en què creu tothom.
Sí que la sabien llarga, aquests! Immenses,
carregades d'electricitat estàtica,
palpitants com una esfinx, les seves vides
donen fe que el més real és el que es calla.

Two Comedians, 1965

Their finale brought to the fore their profession
of loyalty to each other, as well as cellular
oxidation and the most unforeseeable
pathologies and accordion pleats
in skin that was cracking like arid soil.
To be with each other, even to feel
the urge to be the other and crash through
hedges and make the difficult easy as pie
and find each other charming and discerning—
to delight themselves once and for all
they agreed to mutual recognition
owing to a temperament that gravitates
towards order and modern rationality,
and they experienced a change of taste
and put to work a sense of humor
able to laugh at a historical moment
fitted out with civil conscience,
everything the public seeks
and tremendous lost opportunities.
A dirty business. Downcast but undaunted,
heading down for the count but smiling,
they always possessed a gift for farce,
commensurate with themselves.
                                    The con
is the only authentic art, the perfect formula
for egging on every mothers' son to applaud you.
When on one occasion they were asked
about what they believed in, they replied
that everyone believes in the same things.
Those two sure knew what they were doing!
Colossal, charged with static electricity,
fluttering like a sphinx, their lives attest
that what is most real is passed over in silence.

Epilogue: Universalist Church, Gloucester, 1926

Sedentarisme

Nosaltres no prestem atenció
a la salmòdia provinciana
que s'estén pels carrers com ens havien
promès, i no sabem com hem de prendre'ns-ho
o si ens podria fer cap mal. Vosaltres
compreneu el que ens és incomprensible.

A nosaltres no ens ve la suor al front
i això que els contratemps ja estan servits.
A vosaltres us fa pensar en desenes
de processons.
                    Nosaltres no sentim
ni tan sols curiositat pels patis,
els terrats i les golfes de la vora
ni esgarrifances per l'exagerat
repic de les campanes de l'església
que transporta un cop d'aire fins aquí.
Vosaltres esteu plens de sentiment.

Nosaltres no ens en recordem: si encaixen
els últims fets vol dir que ho vèiem clar,
que no calia corregir la lògica.
Una predestinació mistèrica
plana sobre les viles i vosaltres
doneu a entendre que la clau dels fils
dels quals pengem serà que siguin forts.

Epilogue: Universalist Church, Gloucester, 1926

Sedentariness

We pay no heed
to provincial psalmody
swelling through the streets as they
promised us, and we do not know how to grasp it
or whether it might do us harm. You
understand what surpasses our understanding.

On our brow sweat does not bead
even though mischance has befallen us.
To your mind it brings a multitude
of processions.
                We do not feel
the least curiosity about the yards,
roofs and attics nearby
nor do we shudder at the extravagant
pealing of church bells
which stirs the air as far as here.
You are replete with feeling.

We do not remember: if our last deeds
tally, it means our sight is true
and the logic needed no correction.
A predestination as in a mystery cult
hovers over the towns and you
give us to understand the clew of thread
whence we hang shall be as strong as it shall be.

Notes

The Catalan texts are reproduced from Ernest Farrés's book *Edward Hopper: Cinquanta poemes sobre la seva obra pictòrica* (*Fifty poems on his pictorial work*; Barcelona: Viena, 2006). The poem that stands as the epilogue, "Sedentarisme" ("Sedentariness"), was written especially for the Princeton anthology *The Museum as Muse* (2008).

The information supplied in the following notes is culled from my correspondence with Farrés, from Hopper's writing and conversation, and from the diaries and record books kept by his wife, the painter Josephine Nivison Hopper. I have learned much about the Hoppers from Gail Levin's work, particularly her catalogue raisonné and her *Edward Hopper: An Intimate Biography* (New York: Rizzoli, 2007). The interviews with Hopper in the *Time* cover story, "The Silent Witness" (24 December 1956, pp. 28–39), and in Katharine Kuh's *The Artist's Voice: Talks with Seventeen Artists* (New York: Harper & Row, 1962) have also proven helpful.

The notes are intended to reconstruct what might be called the unacknowledged conditions of the paintings, poems, and translations. The aim is to illuminate the intricate network of relations between them, their continuities as well as their disjunctions. Hence the material includes biographical details, identifications of allusions, and the artists' comments on the circumstances and significance of Hopper's paintings.

I have also added quotations that document my use of the Hoppers' language in the translations. For this exercise in lexicography, I chose to omit any definitions for words and phrases, even in cases where the passage of time might have rendered them less familiar or obscure. These items strike me as more revealing if the immediate contexts, however fragmentary, are allowed to shape meanings and to sketch narratives.

Self Portrait, 1925–1930

Farrés's poem alludes not only to the Argentine writer Jorge Luis Borges (1899–1986), but to the American critic Harold Bloom's discussion of Borges's work in *The Western Canon: The Books and School of the Ages* (New

York: Harcourt Brace, 1994). Of particular relevance are two of Borges's stories, "The Theologians" and "The Immortal." In the first, Aurelian of Aquileria and John of Pannonia, both invented church doctors, compete in refuting heresies, and the narrative ends "in Paradise," as James E. Irby's translation reads, where "Aurelia learned that, for the unfathomable divinity, he and John of Pannonia (the orthodox believer and the heretic, the abhorrer and the abhorred, the accuser and the accused) formed one single person." The second story, a fantastic meditation on immortality and the identity of Homer, also concludes with a suggestive passage: in Irby's translation, "When the end draws near, there no longer remains any remembered images; only words remain."

Hopper told Kuh that "The man's the work. Something doesn't come out of nothing. [. . .] I don't think I ever tried to paint the American scene; I'm trying to paint myself" (1962).

scads   In a letter inviting an art critic to see her work, Nivison vacillated: "Of course there are skads of reasons why this could never be" (17 April 1943).

Stairway, 1949

This painting represents the stairway in Hopper's childhood home in Nyack. Nivison's entry in the record book describes the image as "a staircase going down to open door & hall lamp suspended. Said memory of a repeated dream of levitation, sailing downstairs & out thru door" (4 April 1949).

letting anybody down   From Saltillo, a town north of Mexico City, Hopper wrote to his dealer that "The food here [. . .] is a terrible let down" (14 August 1943).

Small Town Station, 1918–1920

milestones-to-grind-for   In an article on the American painter John Sloan, Hopper glanced at his own experience as an illustrator: "First the hard grind and the acquiring sufficient technical skill to make a living" (April 1927).

shouldn't like   When Nivison wrote to the Arts Club of Chicago on the occasion of a Hopper retrospective, urging the curator to exclude the foreward that

Alfred Barr had contributed to an exhibition catalogue for the Museum of Modern Art, Hopper himself intervened: "Mr. Barr's article seems adequate to me and I should like to have it included, if that has been your intention" (9 December 1933).

Railroad Sunset, 1929

hopper   Farrés chose the word "tremuja," the Catalan term for the farming device known as a "hopper," because in English it resembles the painter's surname.

Compartment C, Car 293, 1938

Nivison posed for the female figure, noting in her diary that she sat "by night light in a big pokey hat & hair down" (17 March 1938). In the record book she identified the magazines on the seat beside the figure as *Reader's Digest* and *The New Yorker.*

swell   In a letter to the author of the first monograph on his work, Hopper wrote: "I think you did a swell job on me as a Puritan in the Whitney Museum book" (20 November 1931).

Approaching a City, 1946

Hopper commented on this painting in a late interview: "I've always been interested in approaching a big city by train; and I can't exactly describe the sensations. But they're entirely human and perhaps have nothing to do with esthetics. There is a certain fear and anxiety, and a great visual interest in the things that one sees coming into the city" (1960).

jitters   In a letter to friends complaining of New York University's practices as their landlord, Nivison wrote: "Since there is no where else to go—after E.—being there 47 yrs., I try not to have jitters" (24 January 1961).

that's all right   When *Instructor* magazine approached Hopper for permision to reproduce one of his paintings on the cover, he wrote to his dealer: "I am easing them off by shifting the no to you. If you think otherwise that's all right but I'd rather not do it" (21 October 1952).

Shakespeare at Dusk, 1935

knocking off   Nivison noted in her diary that Hopper "had to knock off painting" the day after attending a gallery exhibition because he was so tired from standing (29 February 1956).

East River, c. 1920–1923

The German writer Hermann Hesse entitled his novel *Siddhartha* (1922) after Prince Siddhartha Gautama, Buddha's name before his renunciation of the world. In Sanskrit "siddha" means "acquired" or "accomplished" while "artha" means "aim" or "wealth" so that "siddhartha" is often translated freely as "wish fulfilled."

Farrés's poem alludes to the opening of T. S. Eliot's "The Dry Salvages" (1941), the third section of *Four Quartets* (1943):

> I do not know much about gods; but I think that the river
> Is a strong brown god—sullen, untamed and intractable,
> Patient to some degree, at first recognised as a frontier;
> Useful, untrustworthy, as a conveyor of commerce;
> Then only a problem confronting the builder of bridges.
> The problem once solved, the brown god is almost forgotten
> By the dwellers in cities—ever, however, implacable.
> Keeping his seasons and rages, destroyer, reminder
> Of what men choose to forget. Unhonoured, unpropitiated
> By worshippers of the machine, but waiting, watching and waiting.

The Catalan text rests on a set of biographical symmetries. Born in St. Louis, a city on the Mississippi River, Eliot spent summers on Cape Ann in northeastern Massachusetts and later settled in London. Hopper's native town was Nyack, located on the Hudson River. He later settled in New York City and bought a house on Cape Cod where he and his wife would spend summers. During the nineteenth century Nyack was the site of shoe manufacturing. Farrés was born and raised in Igualada, a town on the Anoia River in Catalunya; he later went to Barcelona to study and work. Igualada is known for the manufacture of textiles (cotton, linen, wool) and leather, among other products.

pretty   In a letter to his dealer Hopper commented on the "interesting hills" around Saltillo, adding that "It is pretty hard to get near them or do much of anything without a car" (14 August 1943).

Early Sunday Morning, 1930

Hopper told Kuh that this painting "was almost a literal translation of Seventh Avenue [in New York City]," although "it wasn't necessarily Sunday. That word was tacked on later by someone else" (1962).

comport myself   In a letter to his mother describing a "fete" in Paris, Hopper observed that "Given the same liberties, I am afraid that an American crowd would not comport itself so well" (11 May 1907).

Manhattan Bridge Loop, 1928

The Catalan phrase "per Sant Martí" refers to the persistence of warm weather in late fall, what is called "Indian summer" in English. The saint's feast day is celebrated on 11 November.

"what comes to pass"   When a potential buyer once inquired about a specific kind of watercolor, Hopper replied: "I am sure I do not know when such a one will come to pass" (25 November 1956).

The Circle Theatre, 1936

sweat blood   Declining an invitation to contribute to an art magazine, Hopper explained: "I sweat blood when I write" (10 December 1926).

damn foolishness   When Nivison complained to an editor about the reproductions of Hopper's work in an art magazine, the painter wrote to express his disagreement with her: "I have just learned of a damn fool letter that my wife sent you regarding the Arts Portfolio on my stuff" (29 April 1930).

for   In response to a request for a painting from the Whitney Museum, Hopper wrote: "It's very likely that it will be my only new canvas, for I have painted but one this past winter" (30 May 1950).

pals   To a letter addressed to his dealer Hopper added: " 'My best pal and severest critic' sends her best regards and I do also" (6 July 1926).

Night Windows, 1928

D. H. Lawrence's novel *Lady Chatterley's Lover* first appeared in 1928, published privately in Florence in a limited edition of 1000 copies. Its sexual content set off an immediate controversy, and a string of unauthorized editions followed.

The origins of the poet and painter Pere Serafí (c. 1505–1567) are obscure, regarded by some as Greek, by others as Italian. He was based in Barcelona and wrote in both Castilian and Catalan, influenced by Petrarch as well as the medieval Catalan poet Ausiàs March. A characteristic poem included in *Cançons de Pere Serafí* (Barcelona: La Ilustració Catalana, 1905) ends with following stanza (rendered somewhat freely here so as to create a similar prosody):

Bella, si vos ma voluntat	If for certain you might know
sabesseu certa,	what I desire, Fair,
no'm mostraríau crueltat	cruelty you would not show,
tant descuberta;	especially laid so bare;
y jo per vostre gentil cos	for your gentle bod and grace
y galanía,	my sighs will brook no stay,
sempre sospir quant pens en vos	when my thoughts on you I place
la nit y día.	be it night or day.

creepiness   After undergoing surgery Hopper presented his doctors with some of his old drawings and watercolors, telling Nivison that these works "gave him the creeps" (14 January 1958).

Hotel Room, 1931

Nivison's diary entry on this painting refers to her "posing in a pink shimmy shirt far from the fire place (in a bitter cold room) because E. needed the light on the surface of the bed & top of my head, or whatever—& I must endure" (12 April 1960).

Leni Riefenstahl made her Nazi propaganda film *Triumph of the Will* in 1934.

Morning Sun, 1952

germ   In a letter to the editor of an art journal (1935), Hopper wrote:

> In every artist's development the germ of the later work is always found
> in the earlier. The nucleus around which the artist's intellect builds his
> work is himself: the central ego, personality or whatever it may be called,
> and this changes little from birth to death. What he was once, he always
> is, with slight modification.

Summertime, 1943

The ancient Greek philosophers Pyrrho (c. 360–270 BCE) and Gorgias
(c. 487–376 BCE) shared an interest in arguments that challenged a com-
monsensical approach to the world. The skeptic Pyrrho advocated the jux-
taposition of conflicting points to force a suspension of judgment. Gorgias
was known for his rhetorical innovations which included paradoxical forms
of argumentation.

a hard business   In his interview with Kuh (1962), Hopper commented on a
remark about painting made at symposium:

> a member of the "new academy" said that "it" just comes from the
> heart through the arms, through the fingertips, onto the canvas. Now
> some of it does come from the heart, but it has to be amplified by cere-
> bral invention. It's not as easy as just coming through the fingertips. It's
> a hard business.

Nighthawks, 1942

This painting, Hopper told Kuh, "was suggested by a restaurant on Greenwich
Avenue [in New York City]. *Nighthawks* seems to be the way I think of a night
street." When Kuh interjected, "Lonely and empty?" Hopper continued: "I
didn't see it as particularly lonely. I simplified the scene a great deal and made
the restaurant bigger. Unconsciously, probably, I was painting the loneliness
of a large city" (1962).

Nivison described the figures in the record book: "Very good looking boy
in white (coat, cap) inside counter. Girl in red blouse, brown hair eating a

sandwich. Man nighthawk (beak) in dark suit, steel gray hair, black band, blue shirt (clean) holding cigarette. Other figure dark sinister back—at left" (1942).

lousy   Hopper expressed his dislike of illustration in the *Time* cover story: "Sometimes I'd walk around the block a couple of times before I'd go in, wanting the job for money and at the same time hoping to hell I wouldn't get the lousy thing" (24 December 1956).

got   An artist who visited Hopper in the hospital during 1966 recalled him asking, "You got good light?"

Summer in the City, 1949

Nivison's diary (6 December 1949) includes a detailed commentary on this painting:

> He [Hopper] was saying regarding his buxom prima donna for whom I couldn't be used to pose: "C'est le propre de animeaux d'être triste après l'amour"—a fine name for his picture. He says it could scare off buyers. The tall man stretched out head buried in the pillow is a swell piece of improvisation—with no model at all—those long bare legs and feet—hot A.M. after a hot night in the city. But this is going to be another social consciousness picture. E. takes no active interest in social welfare.

Gail Levin has rendered the French: "It is the nature of animals to be gloomy after love."

Excursion into Philosophy, 1959

In her diary Nivison described the male figure as having "a book of Plato on couch, resorted to on morning after episode with young woman who didn't wear Duncan Sandals—not that kind. She an addict to 4" spikes, according to E.H." (written in November 1959). In a letter to an art critic she observed that "a nice girl wouldn't have the soles of her feet so grimy" (23 September 1959). Her entry in the record book added that the Plato was "reread too late."

The ancient Greek thinkers that Farrés names in the poem—Plato and Aristotle, Zeno and Epicurus—have exerted an enormous influence on modern philosophical speculation in various areas, metaphysics and epistemology, aesthetics and ethics.

Girlie Show, 1941

Nivison wrote to Hopper's sister: "Ed beginning a new canvas—a burlesque queen doing a strip tease—and I posing without a stitch on in front of the stove—nothing but high heels in a lottery dance pose" (21 February 1941).

Ludwig Wittgenstein's *Tractatus Logico-Philosophicus* was published in a bilingual German-English edition in 1922. In it he sought to develop a clear and precise foundation for thinking about the relations between reality, language, and thought, although in the end the work narrowed the possible scope of philosophical knowledge.

Office at Night, 1940

Hopper initially entitled this painting *Time and a Half for Over Time, Etc.* while his dealer's assistant proposed *Cordially Yours; Room 1506.*

lonely   In a letter dated 25 August 1948 Hopper explained:

> The picture was probably first suggested by many rides on the "L" train in New York City after dark glimpses of office interiors that were so fleeting as to leave fresh and vivid impressions on my mind. My aim was to try to give the sense of an isolated and lonely office interior rather high in the air, with the office furniture which has a very definite meaning for me.

fishes   Nivison's diary entry describes the image as "a business office with older man at his desk & a secretary, female fishing in a file cabinet. I'm to pose for the same tonight in a tight skirt—short to show legs. Nice that I have good legs & up & coming stockings" (1 February 1940).

New York Restaurant, c. 1922

In a letter written some years later Hopper described his aim in this painting: "In a specific and concrete sense the idea was to attempt to make visual the crowded glamour of a New York restaurant during the noon hour. I am hoping that ideas less easy to define have, perhaps, crept in also" (9 January 1937).

Summer Evening, 1947

In the record book Nivison described the female figure as "standing out for matrimony" (3 October 1947).

Western Motel, 1957

Nivison's entry in the record book refers to the window in this painting as "that glass front of our fine Lloyd Wright guest house" when Hopper and she spent six months in California at the Huntington Hartford Foundation (22 July 1957). She described the female figure as a "haughty blond in dark red, her Buick outside window green." The Hoppers owned a 1954 green-and-white Buick.

scared stiff   Facing the prospect of an acceptance speech for an award from the National Institute of Arts and Letters, Hopper wrote to the president: "I shall be scared stiff upon addressing all those faces, either critical or uncritical, as I have never before spoken to so many" (1 January 1955).

perched   While Hopper was painting *Sunlight on Brownstones,* Nivison described the changes in the female figure in her diary: "He had such an attractive young thing perched on the railing but he's now made her much too old & determined to be perching on that rail & wearing her dark hair down on her shoulders" (28 March 1956).

Solitude, 1944

When this painting was underway, Nivison noted in her diary that Hopper was "working persistently on a lonely house on empty road, sitting in tall grass & not one other earthly thing except a few trees purposely not putting themselves forward," adding that "It would seem almost a stunt to see how far one can eliminate & get only a mood. He early took the pink out of the grass so no one could find there any pretty color" (23 October 1944).

Although Hopper and Nivison relied on their car not only for errands and travel but for transportation to the sites they painted, he rarely allowed her to drive, and their repeated arguments sometimes esclated into violence. In a letter to a friend (8 September 1950) Nivison explained how their contention over driving had resulted in an accident:

> Last week, he grabbed the wheel out of my hands & ran into a post, bending it over & loudly blaming me. Then dragged me out of driver's seat—& all so publicly (cause I clung to the wheel & have black & blue spots to show his talons, post did nothing). Not that I mind all this— this little sop to principle, I'll bruise for principles.

Four Lane Road, 1956

As Hopper worked on this painting Nivison commented in her diary that "The man sits in the sun bearing witness in quiet peace but the wife at the window is more vocal," but then she perceived that Hopper was "making the most evil face on woman at window of filling station in his picture—a regular shrike, expressive of what he's feeling about me" (8 and 10 October 1956). She added that the female figure "finds his serenity a trial."

Wang Wei (701–761) produced one of the great collections of classical Chinese poetry. Farrés's poem alludes to a Chinese text that David Hinton has translated into English as "Bird-Cry Creek" in his book *The Selected Poetry of Wang Wei* (New York: New Directions, 2006):

> In our idleness, cinnamon blossoms fall.
> In night quiet, spring mountains stand
>
> empty. Moonrise startles mountain birds:
> here and there, cries in a spring gorge.

The gift that Hopper gave Nivison for her birthday in 1949 carried the inscription: "à la petite Xanthippe qui le bon Dieu, dans sa sagesse, m'a donné comme femme"—in Gail Levin's rendering, "to the little Xanthippe whom the good Lord, in his wisdom, gave me as a wife."

Hills, South Truro, 1930

pot-boilers "When I am through with the pot-boilers I have on hand," wrote Hopper to a mentor, "I am going at it [i.e., making prints] in earnest" (27 March 1917).

punk Writing from South Truro to a friend Hopper remarked that "I have one canvas and am starting another and have a few punk water colors" (23 July 1930).

Cape Cod Morning, 1950

In a *Time* interview Nivison described the figure in this painting as "a woman looking out to see if the weather's good enough to hang out her wash," but Hopper strongly disagreed: "Did I say that? You're making it Norman Rockwell. From my point of view she's just looking out the window, just looking out the window" (30 May 1955).

Cape Cod Afternoon, 1936

Nivison's diary describes the difficult circumstances under which Hopper painted this work, especially the changing weather conditions (28 October 1936):

> Poor Eddy has had such a dire time finishing his big canvas begun 2 months ago—& so interrupted by downpours & grey weather. The trees lost all their foliage & and the sun changed its position so the long shadows all moved off in other places. He's had to wait for a sky. And when it came he was so tortured by mosquitoes—he standing in high grass & and they getting up his nose even—nearly frantic—& and sun in his eyes—couldn't see what he was doing or tell what it looked like until he got it in doors. But it is lovely.

Cape Cod Sunset, 1934

broke loose "Puzzled" by an art critic's anecdote that used Hopper's conservative taste in clothes to illustrate his "Puritan" personality, the painter responded in a letter: "It has given me courage however in my dress, and I've just broken loose with a very brilliant black tie" (21 November 1931).

The Lighthouse at Two Lights, 1929

works　A caption for a caricature Hopper drew of his wife reads: "There's a virgin—give her the works" (c. 1932).

Lighthouse Hill, 1927

beat it　Hopper told a *Time* interviewer (August–September 1956) an anecdote about a trip to South Carolina:

> There was this cabin back in the woods, and I stopped to sketch it. This mulatto girl came out of the cabin and she seemed interested in what I was doing. Then her husband came home. He was drunk or something and he was going to do something. I don't know what. I beat it.

The Latin words "Beatus ille" (in a close rendering, "Happy is that man") open Horace's second *Epode,* in which a usurer describes the attractions of rural life only to abandon his vision in the end and return to moneylending.

Rooms by the Sea, 1951

In the record book Nivison described the house depicted in this painting as "nothing of the palatial tourist camp. 'Jumping Off Place' for name, turned down—but malign overtones ascribed by some" (7 October 1951).

The Latin phrase "Ex Oriente lux" (literally "light from the East") is an ancient adage that treats Eastern cultures as the preeminent source of knowledge.

nicer　Hopper wrote to his dealer from Saltillo: "It has a nice climate" (14 August 1943).

Sea Watchers, 1952

stack up　In describing his prints to a mentor Hopper wrote: "Hoping they stack up well but feel they are very slight and do not represent me as yet" (27 March 1917).

stinks　Nivison noted in her diary that when she asked Hopper, "Isn't it nice to have a wife who paints?" he replied: "It stinks" (10 September 1941).

The Christian ascetic Simeon the Stylite (c. 390–459) practiced various mortifications of the flesh until, in an effort to escape the pilgrims who sought his advice, he chose to live on a platform atop a pillar for nearly four decades.

Two Comedians, 1965

This painting was Hopper's last. In *Edward Hopper* (New York: Harry Abrams, 1971) the art historian Lloyd Goodrich described it as "a personal testament; the tall male comedian and the small female comedian whom he is presenting to the public are obviously himself and Jo Hopper—a fact which she herself confirmed to me."

Acknowledgments

This project benefited greatly from consultations with the poet, Ernest Farrés, who patiently answered my many questions about his poems and about Catalan poetry generally. I am pleased to record his unstinting help and his unqualified support, even when my choices constituted significant departures from his Catalan texts. Dolors Juanola shared with me her expert knowledge of Catalan philology as I puzzled out various phrases and expressions. Her enthusiastic explanations were inspiring and drove me deeper into the poems. Neither Farrés nor Juanola can be held responsible for what I finally made of their information (even if they share a complicity with the result).

I was fortunate in bringing early drafts of the translations to the attention of sensitive readers who responded with comments that were both appreciative and helpful: Randall Couch, Lisa Dillman, Toby Olson, Caterina Riba Sanmartí, Edward Tayler, and Elizabeth Willis. For indispensable assistance with research, at a great distance, I am indebted to Nick Moudry. My introduction, as well as my translating, was aided by Gary Shapiro's essay, "The Absent Image: Ekphrasis and the 'Infinite Relation' of Translation" (*Journal of Visual Culture* 6/1 [2007]: 13–24), and by the chapter on free verse in James Longenbach's book, *The Resistance to Poetry* (Chicago: University of Chicago Press, 2004).

Grateful acknowledgment is made to the magazines that kindly included some of the translations in their pages: *Boston Review, Calque, Circumference, Crazyhorse, International Literary Quarterly, The Literary Review, The Nation, PN Review, Poetry Wales, Raritan, Subtropics, Two Lines, Words without Borders, World Literature Today,* and *Zoland Poetry.* Other translations appeared in two anthologies: Jan Greenberg's *Side by Side: New Poems Inspired by Art from Around the World* (New York: Harry Abrams, 2008) and Paul Muldoon's *The Museum as Muse* (Princeton: Princeton Art Museum and Program in Creative Writing, 2008).

My work on this translation was greatly advanced by a fellowship from the John Simon Guggenheim Memorial Foundation.

Martha Tennent shared the pains and pleasures of my first foray into the translation of Catalan literature. I could not have done without her encouragement and her tact.

L. V.
Barcelona
June 2008

Born in 1967 in the Catalunyan town of Igualada, **Ernest Farrés** studied journalism at the Universitat Autònoma de Barcelona. He then pursued a doctorate in contemporary Catalan literature at the Universitat de Barcelona, but left before taking the degree to embark on a career as journalist. He wrote for newspapers and magazines before joining the staff of *La Vanguardia*, where he currently works as an editor for the weekly supplement, *Cultura/s*. He is the author of three books of poems, including *Edward Hopper* (2006), which won the Englantina d'Or dels Jocs Florals of Barcelona. He has also edited the anthology *21 poetes del XXI* (2001). His poems have been translated into Spanish and Italian. *Edward Hopper* has been adapted to the stage in Catalan and Spanish.

Lawrence Venuti is a translation theorist and historian as well as a translator from Italian, French, and Catalan. He is the author of *The Translator's Invisibility: A History of Translation* (2008) and *The Scandals of Translation: Towards an Ethics of Difference* (1998). He also edited *The Translation Studies Reader* (2004). His articles and reviews have appeared in such publications as the *Times Literary Supplement* and *Words without Borders*. His translations include Antonia Pozzi's *Breath: Poems and Letters* (2002), the anthology *Italy: A Traveler's Literary Companion* (2003), and Massimo Carlotto's crime novel *The Goodbye Kiss* (2006). He has received awards from the National Endowment for the Arts, the National Endowment for the Humanities, and the Guggenheim Foundation. In 1999 he held a Fulbright Lectureship at the Universitat de Vic.

The text of *Edward Hopper* has been set in Arno Pro, a typeface designed by Robert Slimbach. Book design by Rachel Holscher. Composition by BookMobile Design and Publishing Services, Minneapolis, Minnesota. Manufactured by Versa Press on acid-free paper.